VIRGINIA

An Illustrated History

Illustrated Histories from Hippocrene

VIRGINIA

An Illustrated History

DEBORAH WELCH

HIPPOCRENE BOOKS, INC.
New York

For information address:
  Hippocrene Books, Inc.
  171 Madison Avenue
  New York, NY 10016
  www.hippocrenebooks.com

Cataloging in Publication data available from the Library of Congress.

ISBN 0-7818-1115-5

Printed in the United States of America.

To Peter

Gvgeyui Nigohilvi

Acknowledgements

Alyssa Holland, a 2004 graduate in history at Longwood University and a magnificent research assistant deserves to be singled out for her contributions to this book. Most of the historic photographs contained in these pages were secured by Alyssa who spent long hours digging through collections in state and federal archives as well as private foundation holdings, making copies of many possible reproductions and offering advice of those shots she thought most worthy. Her professor soon learned to rely on her judgment.

Thanks are also owed to Dr. David J. Coles, whose research lies in the Civil War. David was invaluable in suggesting sources and offering details about various battles fought in Virginia, even providing directions to sites he recommended I visit. Barbara Shepard supplied detailed insight into the Randolphs and the practice of slavery in eighteenth-century Virginia. On our campus Professor Shepard's innate ability to bring history alive in the classroom is well known, a contagious enthusiasm she generously shares with the rest of us. Similarly, Dr. James Crowl and Mrs. Pearl Agee offered support and encouragement at every step. Having these colleagues on hand provided ready access to an incredible wealth of information. I took careful notes, but any mistakes found in the pages that follow are the responsibility of the author. I am grateful to Bevin Alexander, another colleague who first introduced me to Hippocrene Books.

Many of the students who pursued public history concentrations at Longwood University contributed photographs to this book, including Kathren Barnes, Sherry L. Livingston, Kathryn M. Blackwell, Dana Luck, John Young, Rachael Blair, and Landace Lowe. The preservation of Virginia's past now lies in the very capable hands of the next generation; people like Alyssa Holland, now undertaking graduate studies in history, Kathryn M. Blackwell who works at the Library of Congress, and Sherry L. Livingston who has written two successful National Register nominations, securing federal protection for the Wade Site in Charlotte County and Fort Hill in Halifax County. They represent the best of Virginia as the Commonwealth moves forward in the twenty-first century.

Foreword

From the Chesapeake Bay to the Blue Ridge Mountains, from Mount Vernon to Monticello, the sights of the Old Dominion have captivated Virginians and visitors alike for centuries. *Virginia: An Illustrated History* commemorates the beauty of the

Mark R. Warner, Governor of the Commonwealth of Virginia from 2002–2006.

Commonwealth and provides insights into the history of the place where the English first permanently settled in the "New World," with the aid of the Indian tribes.

Virginia's rich history can be seen in its early contributions to our nation, from the ideals of freedom espoused in Thomas Jefferson's Declaration of Independence to the selfless service of Virginians during the Revolutionary War. This book acknowledges the bad with the good, and provides us with a valuable lens through which we can look back on Virginia's past. Virginia's storied tradition of excellence in education continues to this day, as the Commonwealth strives to maintain one of the finest education systems in the country. Virginia prides itself on stable and responsible governance, and has held an AAA bond rating longer than any state in the country.

The Commonwealth's unique heritage is a source of pride for Virginians, and it is through reflections such as this book that we can best share our history. We encourage all to explore Virginia beyond the pages of this book.

Mark R. Warner,
Governor of the Commonwealth of Virginia
from TK-2005

Table of Contents

Introduction to the Old Dominion

Virginia, one of the oldest and most beautiful of America's states, lies on the East Coast between Maryland and the District of Columbia to its north, with North Carolina and Tennessee to its south. The Atlantic Ocean and Chesapeake Bay mark Virginia's eastern edge. The state lines of West Virginia and Kentucky form the jagged western border. From the beaches of the Chesapeake Bay through the horse country of the rolling Piedmont and Shenandoah Valley to the Blue Ridge Mountains beyond, it is a land of incomparable beauty, its green valleys memorialized in song by covered-wagon pioneers heading westward across the flat, brown, and often frightening prairies:

> *Oh Shenandoah, I long to hear you,*
> *Far away, you rolling river*
> *Oh Shenandoah, I long to hear you*
> *Away, I'm bound away*
> *'Cross the wide Missouri*

King Charles II first bestowed the name "Old Dominion" on the Virginia colony in recognition of its loyalty to the English crown. Virginia has other commonly used names, including "the Cavalier State," another reminder of its loyalty to the Crown during the English Civil Wars, and one later adopted by post–American Civil War writers of historical fiction to portray a highly romanticized picture of the antebellum South. Today, any mention of the "Cavaliers" invariably involves a discussion (heated debate during football season)

1

A monument at Berkeley Plantation commemorating Union Brigadier General Daniel Butterfield. Gen. Butterfield composed the official call for "Taps" in 1962, while encamped here.
CREDIT: Alyssa Holland

about University of Virginia sports teams. Modern-day Virginians generally refer to "the Commonwealth," a title adopted on June 29, 1776, in Virginia's first state constitution. Less common today, but still to be found in older textbooks, are references to Virginia as "the Mother of States." In its early charters, the colony of Virginia extended from the Atlantic to the Mississippi, encompassing present-day West Virginia, Kentucky, Ohio, Illinois, Wisconsin, Indiana, and even parts of Minnesota. Most certainly, Virginia can still lay claim to its title as "the Mother of Presidents." Eight United States presidents have hailed from Virginia, more than from any other state— George Washington, Thomas Jefferson, James Madison, James Monroe, William Henry Harrison, John Tyler, Zachary Taylor, and Woodrow Wilson.

Above all, Virginians take pride in their historical role as "first" in so many parts of American history. Indeed, William Byrd, an early colonial leader, once wrote, "In the beginning, all America was Virginia."[1] While this defiantly English point of view ignores Indian land claims as well as both Spanish and French territory, his observation, nonetheless, encapsulates a kernel of truth. From its beginnings as the first English colony in America to its present-day role as home to a significant portion of the United States Armed Forces, Virginia has played a central role in American history.

This claim of being at the forefront of so much of United States history begins with the first English settlements founded on Roanoke Island in the 1580s (today part of the North Carolina coast, but organized in the sixteenth century as part of the colony named for Elizabeth I, the "Virgin Queen"). The Indian peoples who populated the land of Virginia, notably the Powhatan Confederacy, were among the first to die in the wave of disease and warfare brought by the invading English. Smallpox, measles, diphtheria, whooping cough, mumps—all proved devastating to a native population with no immunity to the viral infestations the English brought with them.

Jamestown, the first permanent English colony in North America, founded in the Peninsula region of Virginia along the Chesapeake Bay, gave rise to the myth of Pocahontas and John Smith so well known to every American schoolchild. Virginia organized the first non-Indian legislative assembly in the Western world at Jamestown in 1619. Ironically, in that same year, the first African-Americans landed at Jamestown, ostensibly as servants, but the descent into slavery began soon enough. Three years later, in 1622, Virginia was also the scene of the first massive Indian resistance to English encroachments on their territory as the Powhatan peoples led by Opechancanough began an attack on Good Friday, March 22, killing over 350 settlers. English retaliation was swift and merciless as the army raided Indian villages, forcing native peoples off their lands and confining them in the mountainous regions of the Appalachians in a succession of campaigns throughout the seventeenth century. Thus the pattern of future United States Indian Policy (removal and confinement on undesirable land to the west) was first implemented in the Virginia colony—a precedent in which Virginia can take no pride.

Throughout the colonial period, Virginia also remained the largest in territory, population, and, as a result, influence. In many ways, Virginia set the tone of political and social development as the United States first formed and grew. One of the first institutions for higher education in America, the College of William and Mary, was founded in Virginia in 1693. Hampden-Sydney College, one of the two all-male institutions of higher learning remaining in the United States today, organized in 1776. Many additional schools were founded during the Early National period—the University of Virginia (designed by Thomas Jefferson in 1819), Longwood University (first organized as Farmville Female Seminary in 1839), Mary Baldwin College (opening as Augusta Female Seminary in 1842) are among the more than one hundred academies and institutes of higher education that opened in Virginia prior to the Civil War.

The founding fathers unanimously agreed that an educated population was necessary to a successful democracy; indeed, this precept lay at the core of the republican virtue ideal. Virginia led the way in educating its population to fulfill its self-governing role.

Virginia began moving the nation westward when Alexander Spotswood blazed his trail across the mountains into the Shenandoah Valley in 1716. It was a Virginian, Governor Robert Dinwiddie, who precipitated the French and Indian War by sending a force to challenge French claims to the Ohio River Valley. The seeds of discontent and misunderstanding between colonies and mother country sowed by that war would lead to the American Revolution only a few years later.

Virginians have always been proud of the tradition of leadership established by their famous statesmen, many of whom were at the forefront of the Revolution—George Washington, Richard Henry Lee, Edmund Randolph, and Thomas Jefferson among others. It was the "Rump Session" of the Virginia House of Burgesses who, in defiance of the royal governor, first called for a meeting of all of the colonies in 1774 to protest British tyranny, a gathering that became the First Continental Congress. A Virginian, Patrick Henry, provided a rallying cry with his memorably fiery phrase, "Give me liberty or give me death." Another Virginian, Thomas Jefferson, wrote the Declaration of Independence, outlining the reasons why this new nation must separate itself from Great Britain. Equally important, it was Jefferson who so eloquently outlined the necessity of separation of church and state, a guiding hallmark of American liberty, in his "Act for Establishing Religious Freedom."[2]

A Virginian, Richard Henry Lee, first called for debate on the issue of declaring independence in the Second Continental Congress, thus paving the way for the colonies to vote on Jefferson's declaration and commit themselves to war. Another Virginian, George Washington, led the Continental Army to

A monument to a Confederate soldier (at right) in a cemetary in Hampton Roads.
CREDIT: Rachael Blair

victory in the American Revolution and went on to become the nation's first president. Finally, it was still another Virginian, James Madison, who, in 1787, played the principal role in crafting a document of government for the new nation, the Constitution.

Virginians were not only at the forefront of creating this nation but also played an important part in expanding its borders. The Louisiana Purchase, which doubled the size of the country in 1803, ensuring that the United States would ultimately be a two-ocean country, was secured from France and its acquisition pushed through Congress by Thomas Jefferson. President Jefferson then sent two of his fellow Virginians, William Clark and Meriwether Lewis, on the famous

6

expedition that began the opening of the American West to Anglo settlement.

Sadly the sons and grandsons of many of the Virginians who played such pivotal roles in establishing and expanding the United States would later die on the battlefields of the Civil War fighting for a Confederacy seeking to tear apart the Union their forefathers had created. Virginia did not start the Civil War; that lot fell to the "Hotspurs" of South Carolina who first seceded and then fired on Fort Sumter.[3] Nonetheless, it was a son of Virginia, Robert E. Lee, who led the Confederate Army of Northern Virginia and, in a sad irony, it was Virginia and North Carolina, two of the most reluctant states to leave the Union, whose men bore the brunt of the casualties.[4]

Richmond served as the capital of the Confederacy throughout most of the conflict, and many of its most costly battles were fought on Virginia soil. Bull Run, Petersburg, Fredericksburg, Chancellorsville, Cold Harbor, and finally Appomattox are among the better known. Over one hundred major battles and skirmishes bloodied Virginia ground. A significant portion of the Confederacy's best-known generals hailed from Virginia, including Stonewall Jackson, J. E. B. Stuart, James L. Kemper, Jubal A. Early, Henry Heth, Richard S. Ewell, A. P. Hill, Joseph E. Johnston, and Samuel Cooper, among others. General George Pickett, whose name will forever be linked with the suicidal charge on July 3, 1863, at the Battle of Gettysburg, was a native of Richmond. Two of the generals who died as part of that disastrous maneuver, Lewis A. Armistead and Richard S. Garnett, were also Virginians. Lee lost one-third of his army at Gettysburg; Confederate casualties—those killed, wounded, or missing—exceeded twenty-eight thousand men. Still the war would continue for nearly two more bloody years.

Those leaders who led the South out of the Union argued that they did so to protect the Constitution and their individual liberties. But in the end, it was a war about slavery; and Virginia, which had from colonial times enslaved African-Americans, paid a heavy price for the failure of all Americans to find a way to put an end to the South's "Peculiar Institution."

The Civil War destroyed the South's practice of slavery, emancipating approximately four million souls who had been kept in bondage. It also established the primacy of the federal government over the individual states and outlined a future in which the national economy would be based on industry rather than agriculture. In the aftermath of the war, Virginia, like the rest of the New South, turned to a long-overdue development of manufacturing, though one still dependent on the traditional Southern cash crops. Tobacco production and cigarette plants, cotton textile mills, lumber and furniture making—all became hallmarks of the late nineteenth- through twentieth-century Virginia economy. As a result, much of Virginia remained rural, its people tied to their land and an agricultural tradition.

In the twentieth century, Virginia continued to rely upon its farmers—primarily of tobacco, grain, cotton, and dairy. In the latter half of the century, tourism became a major industry, with vacationers drawn by the beauty of the state and its long history. Currently, the U.S. military also makes a significant contribution to the area's economy through the operation of a number of military bases throughout the state. Norfolk naval base is home to the Atlantic fleet. The population growth in northern Virginia that resulted from the tremendous expansion of the nation's capital during World War II and the more recent development of high-tech industries are also leading factors in the state's modern economy. And always there have been horses. Some of the finest thoroughbreds in the country are raised on farms in the Piedmont, [in] Shenandoah, and [in] northern Virginia, particularly Loudon County. Virginians are particularly proud of the Chincoteague ponies.

It took decades for Virginia to recover from the Civil War, and the scars remain. Every city, town, and village throughout the Commonwealth has at least one statue commemorating its Civil War dead. Contrary to popular myth, Virginians do not insist on calling the conflict "the War between the States." Nomenclature aside, most of the fighting took place on Virginia soil and it was to Richmond hospitals that the wounded were carried, many of them to die. Hollywood Cemetery in Richmond, where some eighteen thousand soldiers from that conflict are interred, remains a lasting memorial to the determination of Virginians to honor "Our Glorious Dead" and keep alive for decades following the Civil War the myth of "The Lost Cause."

In another "first," Virginia led the way in furthering the historic preservation movement in the United States, beginning in the mid-nineteenth century with the concept of house museums. The Mount Vernon Ladies' Association bought George Washington's home in 1858. In the early twentieth century the Thomas Jefferson Foundation acquired Monticello, opening the house and grounds as a museum and education site. Today, Monticello still rises majestically on its mountain overlooking the University of Virginia at Charlottesville, which Jefferson founded and considered one of his crowning achievements. Monticello stands as the only house in the United States recognized by the United Nations' World Heritage List of sites that must be protected for the future.

In the 1920s and '30s, John D. Rockefeller, Jr. pushed ambitiously forward the concept of preservation with the meticulous reconstruction of Williamsburg. Today, Williamsburg is a living museum visited by thousands of tourists every year. Moreover, its success furthered the preservation movement by spawning similar museum villages throughout the country.

Many of Virginia's historic homes have been preserved and are today open to the public—Montpelier, home of the nation's fourth president, James Madison; Ash Lawn-High-lands, home of the nation's fifth president, James Monroe; Dadona Manor, home of General George C. Marshall; William Byrd's Westover Plantation; and many other majestic estates, "the houses that tobacco built," as well as the homes of noted Civil War generals like Stonewall Jackson. The Virginia Landmarks Register recognizes hundreds of historic sites, most notably the Monument Avenue Historic District in Richmond, as well as museums, historic churches, entrepreneurial edifices, and archeological sites. Many tourists come to visit the battlefields, the majority of which, including Yorktown, Chancellorsville, Fredericksburg, and Appomattox, are overseen by the National Park Service. The state maintains other battlefield sites, such as Saylor's Creek, the last running battle of the war before the end came at Appomattox. Historic markers dot the roadways and visitors may follow the route of Lee's Retreat throughout Virginia. Similar plans are now underway to create a Civil Rights Trail.

While colonial and Revolutionary War locales like Jamestown and Yorktown as well as the many Civil War battlefields draw visitors to Virginia, the state is equally proud of those sites dedicated to the preservation of African-American history. Booker T. Washington, founder and guiding spirit of Tuskegee Institute, was born a slave in Hardy, Virginia—today the site of the Booker T. National Monument. Equally important to both United States and Virginia history is the Robert R. Moton School in Farmville. On April 23, 1951, the black students at Moton staged a unanimous walkout in protest of terribly overcrowded conditions. Their actions resulted one month later in a suit filed by the parents along with the NAACP, *Davis v. Prince Edward County*. That case, bundled with four others, became part of the landmark 1954 Supreme Court *Brown v. Board of Education* decision, overturning the Court's 1896 *Plessy v. Ferguson* "separate but equal" ruling.

The Court's decision marked the beginning of the end of segregation in public schools, but a long battle still lay ahead. Virginia, along with many other states, employed the tactic of "massive resistance," closing its schools rather than accepting black students. Prince Edward County held out the longest, keeping its schools closed from 1959 until 1964. Today, the Robert R. Moton building stands as a national landmark and will be the center of the proposed statewide Civil Rights Trail.

This book tells the stories of many black Virginians, who, no less than their white neighbors, played a significant role in the development of this state, including Carter G. Woodson, founder of the *Journal of Negro History*; Charles S. Johnson, who became president of Fisk University; and other artists, actors, and musicians of whom all of Virginia should be proud.

In the twentieth century, African-Americans have continued Virginia's legacy of being first in the nation. In 1903, Maggie Lena Walker of Richmond became the nation's first African-American female bank president. Her path-breaking achievements both for women and blacks were commemorated in 1937–38 with the building of the Maggie Walker School, a Virginia Landmark. Arthur Ashe remains one of Virginia's most famous sons. His achievements include his having been the first African-American selected to represent the U.S. in Davis Cup play in 1963, and the winner of the U.S. Open in 1968 and Wimbledon in 1975. Ashe's determination to oppose Apartheid in South Africa, and, most especially, the gentle decency with which he conducted his life and faced his untimely death, were recognized when a statue of this Richmond native was added to the city's Monument Avenue. In 1990, Douglas Wilder, a Richmond attorney, became the first African-American governor elected in the United States. In 2002, Leroy R. Hassell was elected by his peers on the Virginia Supreme Court to be its chief justice, the first black man to hold this post and the first chief justice in Virginia history to be elected by his fellow justices.

Skyline Drive in Autumn.
CREDIT: Shenandoah National Park

Today, visitors flock to Virginia at all times of the year. In the winter, they come to the mountains for the wonderful skiing available at resorts like Wintergreen; in the summer, they head for the beaches along Virginia's extensive seashore and visit the magnificent battleships at Norfolk Naval Yard; in the autumn, they are drawn by the brilliant foliage of the Shenandoah Valley and throughout the Blue Ridge. But it is in spring that Virginia is perhaps at its finest. As the gentle green grasses return to the rolling hills of the Piedmont regions, the dogwoods dot the woods with their white and pink blossoms, and the daylilies begin to cover the countryside, Virginia's beauty and vitality are in evidence throughout this state.

The history of Virginia is, in many ways, the history of America, and this is especially striking in the spring. It was in April 1607 that the Jamestown settlers first set foot in North America, beginning English colonization; in April 1619 that the first Africans landed at Jamestown; in April 1861 that Virginia seceded from the Union; in April 1863 that the bloody battle of Chancellorsville began; in April 1865 that the long Civil War came to an end as Lee surrendered to Grant at Appomattox. Finally, it was in April 1951 that those courageous students at Robert R. Moton School staged their walkout, thus precipitating one of the Supreme Court's most famous landmark decisions, setting aside "separate but equal" and mandating integration of the nation's public schools.

Whatever the season, so much of American history took place in Virginia, a history which celebrates its achievements even as it attempts to address the failings of its past. The story of both will be found in the pages that follow, highlighting the people and events that shaped this state. Throughout, the principal theme is one of pride—Southern pride perhaps, but here again, Virginia leads—there is no match for Virginia's pride in its state, its long history, and the vital role it continues to play in America's story.

Notes

1. Carol McGinnis, *Virginia Genealogy: Sources and Resources* (Baltimore: Genealogical Publishing Company, 1993), 1.
2. In an ironic twist of fate, the ownership of Jefferson's beloved home, Monticello, would give rise to a pitched debate in the early twentieth century in which anti-Semitism played a shameful role.
3. However, it was a Virginian, Edward Ruffin who was given the "honor" of firing the first canon at Fort Sumter in April 1861.
4. Indeed, North Carolina, the tenth of the eleven southern states to secede, bore the greatest loss of men, with Virginia following a close second.

Chapter One

The Cavalier State

Virginians often say that they have the beaches for their front yard and the mountains for their back. Probably best known in the popular imagination as the heart of the Old South, Virginia is dotted with historic sites from Jamestown and Yorktown on the coast to the plantation estates that tobacco built along the James River inland, and from Civil War battlefield sites marking horrific conflict at Fredericksburg, Petersburg, Manassas, and elsewhere to the rolling hills of the Piedmont, the beauty of the Shenandoah Valley, and the mountains beyond. It is indeed a state of marked geographic contrasts.

Roughly triangular in shape, Virginia stretches 440 miles along her southern border, which divides her from the states of North Carolina and Tennessee. But that number is misleadingly large. From the Cumberland Gap in the west, the state line separating the Old Dominion from West Virginia and Kentucky begins a jagged but extreme northeastern slant toward the District of Columbia. Running North–South, Virginia is only 196 miles long, but the cosmopolitan world of northern Virginia stands in marked contrast to the agricultural poverty of the region lying below the James River, commonly referred to as the Southside. Northern Virginia—Arlington (the smallest county in the state), Fairfax, Loudon, and Prince William counties—is home to large numbers of people whose livelihood is gained across the Potomac in the nation's capital. Southside Virginia—Nottoway, Prince Edward, Cumberland, Appomattox, Lunenburg, Mecklenburg, Charlotte, and Halifax counties—remains largely rural, a region of small farmers

Shenandoah mountains.
CREDIT: Claire Clauss

who struggle mightily to hold on to a lifestyle rapidly disappearing in the twenty-first century.

In total, Virginia covers 42,767 square miles, 2,365 of which are water. It boasts 567 miles of coastline, 342 on the mainland and another 225 miles on islands. Its highest point, Mount Rogers, stands at 5,719 feet in Smyth and Grayson counties.

Virginia is made up of ninety-five counties, one-quarter bearing the names of English royalty—Prince William, Prince Edward, etc. Still others share British place names, reminders of the state's origins as the first English colony in North America—Essex, Gloucestershire, Norfolk, Northampton, Northumberland, New Kent, Southampton, Stafford, Warwick, Westmoreland, and York; even Richmond, the state capital. In addition to its counties, Virginia's local government includes forty independent cities and 189 incorporated towns.

The state flower is the dogwood, given that designation by the General Assembly in 1918 in recognition of the plentiful trees that bloom every spring throughout the state. Indeed, the earliest English explorers' accounts of Virginia invariably mention the dogwood and sweet-smelling honeysuckle vines they found everywhere in the thick forests. The state flag features a deep blue field, in the center of which lies the state seal along with the motto, *Sic Semper Tyrannis* (Thus Always to Tyrants). By law the flag must be made of bunting or merino and include a white silk fringe on the edge.

Virginia boasts a number of scenic rivers popular with sportsmen, particularly fishermen and those who enjoy canoeing and rafting. The largest of these include the Appomattox, Dan, James, Potomac, Rappahannock, Roanoke, and Shenandoah. Four mountain ranges—the Alleghany, Blue Ridge, Cumberland, and Shenandoah—are separated by scenic valleys that draw flocks of tourists every fall and spring to view the beauty of nature along Skyline Drive and the Appalachian Trail.

The current population of the state exceeds 7 million people. Like the rest of the American South, which industrialized after the Civil War along on a pattern based upon agriculture, setting it apart from the more urbanized North, Virginia has few large cities. Even Richmond possesses a population of only 965,200 people, far smaller than other Southern cities like Atlanta, Charlotte, or New Orleans. The Norfolk, Virginia Beach, and Newport News region, home to the U.S. Atlantic fleet, is considerably larger, with 1,521,000 people. Northern Virginia is, by far, the most densely populated region of the state, with 2,083,700 denizens.

The geography of Virginia is best viewed as eight separate regions. Beginning in the East on the Atlantic, there is the area known as the Eastern Shore. Populated by families who have lived there for generations and value the privacy afforded them by their peninsular/island setting, the Eastern Shore offers quaint towns, wildlife refuges, and, of course, the Chincoteague ponies.

The Hampton Roads area boasts Virginia's best beaches as well as many colonial historic sites, including Jamestown, Yorktown, and Williamsburg. It is also home to the U.S. naval base at Norfolk. Traveling northward, one enters the Chesapeake Bay region, including the peninsula areas known as the Northern and Middle Necks. Stretching from King George to Gloucestershire, these lowlands are home to rural fishing villages, berry farms, and wineries. Boaters are drawn to these waterways and their many natural harbors.

At the top of the state lies Northern Virginia, viewed by many as a bedroom community filled with those who must make the arduous commute daily into Washington, D.C. But it is also the site of Mount Vernon, home of America's first president. At its western edge, Northern Virginia boasts some of the finest horse country in America.

Moving southward into the rolling hills of the Piedmont, one enters central Virginia, roughly that area stretching from the state capital at Richmond to Charlottesville—home of one of the nation's oldest and finest institutions of higher education, the University of Virginia—and south to the North Carolina state line. Famous for its Civil War sites, including Fredericksburg, Petersburg, and Appomattox, all of which are managed by the National Park Service, this region also contains state parks, some of which commemorate lesser-known Civil War battles.

To the west lies the Shenandoah Valley, stretching from Roanoke to Winchester. Famous for its Civil War history as well, this area now draws tourists to its spectacular fall foliage, ski and golf resorts, and arts and crafts. Moving still further to the west, one encounters the Blue Ridge Highlands, home to some of the most beautiful mountains in southern Appalachia.

James River at the rocks in Richmond, VA.
CREDIT: Alyssa Holland

Reached by Interstate 81 or 77, the Highlands are home to Virginia Tech University in Blacksburg.

At the extreme southwestern corner of the state lies an area known as the Heart of Appalachia. This region shares the coal-mining history of neighboring Kentucky and West Virginia. It is also famous for its mountain heritage, especially its music.

Virginia is a state of vast geographic variety, and as a result, also a state of vast cultural variety. While manufacturing, exports, rapidly growing high-tech industries, and agriculture make major contributions to the state's economy, tourism plays a principal role as well. Many people travel to Virginia each year to enjoy its beaches in the Hampton Roads or to view wildlife refuges of the Eastern Shore or to engage in the many sports opportunities available in the Shenandoah Valley and Blue Ridge Highlands.

One of the Old Dominion's principal claims to fame is its horse country. Whether one is interested in thoroughbred racing, polo, or steeplechase jumping, all manner of horse shows can be found in Virginia. Northern Virginia is home to the Middleburg Classic Horse Show each September, featuring horses in arena and field competition. In nearby Upperville, the Hunt Country Stable Tour is conducted in late May. Both the International Gold Cup at the Great Meadows Event Center and the Virginia Gold Cup in Warrenton feature steeplechase races, taking advantage of Virginia's beautiful spring weather every year. The Warrenton Horse Show, held in late August, hosts one of the oldest hunter/jumper shows in the country. Those interested in steeplechase racing should visit the Foxfield races in Charlottesville (held twice yearly in the spring and fall), the Bedford County Hunt Point to Point Races in May, and the Montpelier Hunt Races (on the first Saturday in November). Montpelier, the home of fourth U.S. president James Madison, also hosts the Cleveland Bay Horse Show. This breed, first developed in England as a carriage horse, was imported into Virginia in the early 1800s. Fewer than seven hundred exist today.

Perhaps best known is the Virginia Horse Center in Lexington, a six-hundred-acre facility, including ten show rings, a five mile cross-country course, and an indoor arena with seating for four thousand. Equally deserving of attention are the Chincoteague ponies, made famous in novels and films. Every July, wild ponies from Chincoteague National Wildlife Refuge on Assateague Island are rounded up and swim across the channel to Chincoteague Island. There the largest herd of Misty family descendents may be viewed.

As might be expected in a state populated by so many horses, one of the finest veterinary colleges in the nation is

The Chincoteague Ponies of Assateague Island on Virginia's Eastern Shore.
CREDIT: Allison Turner, National Park Service

located at Virginia Tech, formally known as Virginia Poly-technic Institute and State University. The Virginia-Maryland Regional College of Veterinary Medicine, headquartered at Blacksburg, features three campuses, including the Marion duPont Scott Equine Medical Center in Leesburg.

Virginians love their horses and are particularly proud that they preserved a wild herd found on Assategue Island in the Chesapeake Bay. The history of Virginia did not begin with English settlement, and the Chincoteague ponies are a reminder that this land was home to large numbers of Indian people for thousands of years before any Europeans ventured westward across the Atlantic. Thus it is with the story of American Indian peoples that any history of Virginia must begin.

Chapter Two
Owenvsv

Owenvsv, in the Tsalagi (Cherokee) language, means "home." And the Cherokee, one of the largest nations in the American South at the time of European contact, claimed Virginia as part of their sphere of influence. So did the Haudenosaunee (Iroquois) Confederacy to the north. While these tribes did not recognize property ownership as Europeans understood it—and would seek to impose it—Indian peoples certainly fought each other for domination over lands.

At the time of contact, there were several distinct linguistic groups living in the area of present-day Virginia, in the form of small tribes resisting encroachment from their far more powerful neighbors to the north and to the south. From the coastal regions to the falls near Richmond the palisade towns of thirty to thirty-five Algonquin tribes were loosely tied together until the mantle of the Powhatan Confederacy. Altogether, the population of Powhatan's groups probably numbered around ten thousand people at the start of the seventeenth century. The most powerful of these tribes was the Pamunkey Band, followed by the Rappahannocks.

Beyond the falls, in a vast territory stretching from the Upper James, Potomac, and Rappahannock rivers to the Alleghany Mountains, lived the Monacan and Manahoac federations, Siouan peoples who were enemies of their Algonquin neighbors. They were farmers and fisherman, for the most part, like other Eastern Woodland peoples. Monacan and Manahoac influence stopped at the Shenandoah Valley, an area claimed by many, including the Shawnee, Catawba, and Delaware.

Iroquoian inroads into territory within the borders of modern Virginia were made by the Susquehanna tribe, which lived in the area of the headwaters of Chesapeake Bay. The Rickohockan or Rechahecrian peoples, loosely identified with the Cherokee, lived in the mountain valleys of the Southwest.

It was with the Pamunkey and Rappahannock bands that the English first came into contact. Sixteenth-century English drawings confirm that the Pamunkey and Rappahannock lived in towns, almost always surrounded by a wooden palisade, located on high ground in close proximity to a river or fresh springs. These villages were made up of longhouse-type structures, edifices of bark and rushes. One room surrounded by platforms for sleeping on each side housed up to twenty people. A central fire with a smoke hole cut overhead provided warmth.

The Cherokee people of the southern mountain areas built villages that hugged streams and valleys. They preferred log dwellings, using clay to chink the walls against the cold mountain winds. Sweat lodges and council houses completed their towns.

For centuries, the Indian peoples of Virginia had developed cultures centered around agriculture, developing extensive crops of corn, beans, and squash—referred to as "the Three Sisters" by the Haudenosaunee. Corn seems to have been especially important. Early explorers report large fields under cultivation, complete with mounted platform for watchers to frighten away birds and other wildlife. These Indian people were great fishermen as well, developing ingenious methods of tied-line spearing with arrows, guaranteed to garner a substantial harvest. They also hunted, usually in groups.

Turkey appears to have been a mainstay, and turkey wing bone was highly prized for jewelry making, especially among the Cherokee and Catawba peoples of the west. First fired, the delicate pieces were then painted and sometimes etched for use in pectoral decorations. Among the Algonquin and Siouan

A De Bry engraving of Secotan Village.
CREDIT: Virginia Historical Society

peoples with whom the English first had contact, clamshells and copper pendants were most often noted as popular jewelry as well as feathered headgear.

The extension of Southeastern mound culture is also evident in Virginia, where various tribes often employed techniques later adopted by Plains Indian people, of wrapping a dead body in mats and then putting it on a scaffold three or four yards high. Once stripped of flesh by birds and decay, the bones were gathered and put in pits, eventually forming mounds. This technique of using graves to mark a people's land was common among agricultural societies worldwide.

Virginia Indian peoples were also monotheistic. The Pamunkey referred to God as *Mannith* ("creator") or *Okee*. This shared religious belief did not suit English purposes however. In one of his reports, John Smith wrote that Okee was the Indian word for "devil," whom, he claimed, the savages worshipped. Heathenism provided an excuse for war and land seizure.

From the outset, relations between Virginia's Indian peoples and the Jamestown colony were hostile, with a number of atrocities reported on both sides. The English recognized Powhatan as the most powerful leader, ruling over an extensive area and possessing thirty-six capitals. It was at Werowocomoco, reportedly Powhatan's favorite town on the bank of the York River, that he first encountered John Smith. But Powhatan would be forced to abandon Werowocomoco and withdraw westward, as the English began seizing settlements. Still the fighting was fierce; at one point the colonists even considered abandoning Jamestown.

The marriage of John Rolfe and Powhatan's daughter, Pocahontas in 1614 produced a truce that lasted for eight years. After Powhatan's death, Opechecanough assumed leadership of the confederacy and, on Good Friday 1622, began the war commonly known as the Jamestown Massacre, resulting in the death of 350 settlers. Retaliation throughout the autumn and winter of 1622 was swift and merciless, killing so many of the Pamunkey Band that they were not able to mount further resistance for two decades.

In 1644, an elderly Opechecanough made one last stab at ousting the English settlers, resuming what he must have known was a hopeless fight. He was captured and taken to Jamestown, where he was killed. Two years later, the remaining Pamunkey signed a treaty ceding all lands below the falls of the James and Pamunkey rivers to the Virginia Colony.

English penetration beyond the falls brought them into contact with the Siouan Monacan and Manahoac confederacies. Of far greater concern to these Indian peoples by the mid-seventeenth century were the incursions being made by Iroquois invaders pushing down from New York. The overwhelming force of the Haudenosaunee armies drove the Manahoacs closer to the falls of the James and thus directly into the path of English expansion. Determined the force them away, the Virginia Colony called upon the Pamunkey, long enemies of the Manahoac, to do battle, thus precipitating one of the bloodiest conflicts between Indian peoples on Virginia soil in the late 1650s.

By 1665, the remaining Algonquin tribes were forced to accept their status as Virginia Colony dependents. After the 1684 Albany Treaty, the once powerful Powhatan Confederacy was shattered. Similarly, in 1676, the Susquehanna were driven from the Chesapeake area. By 1705, the Indian population in Virginia numbered no more than five hundred able-bodied men; two-thirds were survivors of the Powhatan Confederacy.

Warfare alone does not account for the decimation of Indian populations during the early colonial period. The principal killer was disease, brought by the invading English unwittingly, with deadly results for a people who had no immunity against smallpox, whopping cough, measles, and a myriad of other European illnesses, which wiped out whole towns.

Within one hundred years of the first English settlement at Jamestown, Indian populations had been so reduced that they were considered negligible by their conquerors.[1]

In the late eighteenth century, only the Shenandoah Valley remained outside English control. This beautiful valley, claimed by many, was the scene of extensive fighting, intensified by the outbreak of the French and Indian War in 1754. Following the Treaty of Paris in 1763, Indian peoples withdrew to the west side of the Appalachian Mountains in accordance with the deal struck by Pontiac, who had led the first pan-Indian military movement in American history against the English. The Proclamation of 1763 drew a line down the middle of the mountains, a boundary between red and white skin. All of Virginia now belonged to the English.

Today there are eight state-recognized tribes living in Virginia. They are small groups of people, some numbering less than one hundred. All eight are incorporated as nonprofit organizations and celebrate their Indian heritage proudly, an option not possible for them until the second half of the twentieth century. After 1913, when birth certificates became mandated by law, the state of Virginia began a systematic policy to erase all Indian identity. Through the 1950s, it remained a state crime for anyone to call himself Indian. That little-known byproduct of the Jim Crow era has passed, but despite the efforts of such Congressmen as Jim Moran, federal recognition still eludes Virginia Indian people. Those tribes are:

The Chickahominy

These were among the first Indian peoples with whom the Jamestown invaders made contact with because of their location on the nearby Chickahominy River. Driven off their lands into King William County near the Mattaponi Reserve, the

Modern Powwow Dance Competitions.
CREDIT: Deborah Welch

Chickahominy soon lost that home as well. Eventually, surviving families began a migration back to the site of one of their original towns at Chickahominy Ridge in Charles City County. There they bought land, where they still remain. Located about midway between Richmond and Williamsburg, the Chickahominy built a tribal center and host powwows as well as a Fall Festival. They, along with five other Virginia Indian groups, received state recognition in 1983.

The Eastern Chickahominy

Also recognized by the state in 1983, the Eastern Band of the Chickahominy reside in New Kent County, about twenty-five miles east of Richmond. Their population is small, numbering only 150 at the last census.

The Mattaponi

In 1646, the Mattaponi began paying tribute to Virginia's colonial governor. These overtures of peace, combined with their small numbers that posed no conceivable threat, convinced their English overlords to allow them to stay on their homeland on the banks of the Mattaponi River in King William County. Also recognized by the state in 1983, the Mattaponi today number no more than seventy-five people.

The Monacan

Far larger, though still small compared to most Indian nations, the Monacan have a population of nine hundred, the descendents of the once mighty Monacan people who, with their Manahoac allies on the Rappahannock River, controlled all of the territory between modern-day Richmond and the Shenandoah. The most western of the state-recognized tribes (receiving that status in 1989), the Monacan have lived on Bear Mountain in Amherst County for over ten thousand years. They remain there today.

The Nansemond

At the time of English contact, the Nansemond lived in several towns on both sides of the Nansemond River (today the city of Suffolk). Their *werowance*, or chief, lived on nearby Dumpling Island. Numbering approximately twelve hundred when the

English arrived, their numbers were quickly decimated by disease. Moreover, they occupied rich farmland, coveted by the Jamestown colonists for tobacco cultivation. The Nansemond were moved several times, losing their last lands in 1791. Today, approximately three hundred of their descendants live in the Chesapeake-Suffolk area.

The Pamunkey

The most powerful tribe of the Powhatan Confederacy, their population has been reduced to only one hundred. They live on a small reserve alongside the Pamunkey River in King William County near West Point, Virginia.

The Rappahannock

The Rappahannock people were targeted as a threat early on by the Jamestown colonists. Captain John Smith first encountered them in 1608 at a place called Cat Point Creek, on the Rappahannock River. A powerful people, they lived in thirteen villages on the north side of the river, with two additional towns on the south banks. But like the rest of Virginia's indigenous peoples, they were driven off their lands, initially relocated to Portabago Indian Town. In 1705, they were forced to move again, this time to a 3,473- acre reserve at Indian Neck in King and Queen County. Their descendants remain there today. Numbering approximately three hundred, the Rappahannock have tried to coexist with Virginia, first incorporating in 1921. More recently, they have begun a tribal cultural center and museum, and have purchased one hundred acres for planned development.

Their annual Harvest Festival is held each year on the second Saturday in October, in Indian Neck, Virginia. They are determined survivors, dedicated to preserving Rappahannock social and political structures while educating new generations of all races about Rappahannock cultural identity.

The Upper Mattaponi

The Upper Mattaponi Tribe has no reservation. Only about one hundred people strong, they are descendents of people drawn from the Mattaponi and Pamunkey bands. Their community is centered around the Indian View Baptist Church and the adjacent Sharon Indian School, built in 1919. Closed in 1964, the school was returned to the tribe by the King William County Board of Supervisors in 1985. Today, it serves as a tribal center.

These eight recognized tribes are represented on the Virginia Council of Indians, a group appointed by the governor, which meets monthly in Richmond to review Indian affairs statewide. Only fifteen members make up this body: one delegate from each of the eight tribes, two Indian members at large, one citizen member at large, three delegates, and one senator from the General Assembly. For more information, they may be contacted at the Virginia Council of Indians, P.O. Box 1475, Richmond, VA 23218.

Note

1. See *Executive Journals of the Council of Colonial Virginia,* 1680s on (London: Public Record Office, Colonial Office, Class 5, beginning with Volume 1405). See also Susan Myra Kingsbury, ed., *The Records of the Virginia Land Company* (Washington: Government Printing Office, 1906). For more information about Virginia

Indian peoples' attempts to achieve federal recognition, see "Virginia's First People," *Southside Electric Cooperative Living* (October 2003): 14–18, 41. This article contains current bills being introduced in Congress by Virginia's representatives as well as contact information for all of the tribes.

Chapter Three
Jamestown

The English colony of Virginia began in what is today the outer banks region of North Carolina. Perhaps more accurately, it was conceived in the imagination of a generation of Englishmen, nowhere more fervently than in the vision of Sir Walter Ralegh. This favorite of the court of Elizabeth I put together the first expedition to establish an English empire in what was, at the end of the sixteenth century, a hemisphere euphemistically called by those who sought to conquer it, the New World.

Many factors combined to foster the onset of English exploration and settlement. The enclosure movement, which turned village commons previously reserved for farming into pasture for wool-producing sheep eliminated the livelihoods of thousands, resulting in a perception of overcrowding in English cities. Most certainly, crime rose at a shocking rate, often at the hands of men desperate to feed their families.

The spirit of adventure and curiosity inherent in the age of the Renaissance also played its role. The legend of Marco Polo still fired men's ambitions, as did the perpetual hope of finding a Northwest Passage, a water route through North America to the riches of the Indies.

The moral obligation to spread Protestantism, the New Learning, among the native peoples of the Americas inspired some settlers. In any event, Anglican-blessed missions of conversion provided useful window dressing to disguise an invasion, the central purpose of which was conquest—a land grab no less destructive to Indian peoples than that undertaken by first the Spanish and later the French invaders. Evangelical aspirations aside, nationality was fast becoming the new religion of the competing nations of Europe, a rivalry intensified by their division into Protestant and Catholic camps as a result of first the Reformation and then the Counter-Reformation. Therefore, it was with an eye to limiting Spanish hegemony over the New World, as much as to countering Catholicism, that Ralegh's first expedition, led by captains Arthur Barlow and Philip Amadas set sail in 1584.

This small group explored the Hatteras coastline, calling the largest island Roanoke from the language of its Indian inhabitants. Native peoples called the nearby mainland Wyngandacoa. Englishmen named all of it Virginia, in honor of Elizabeth, their Virgin Queen.

The following year, a colonizing party set out for Hatteras. But the colony did not fare well, falling prey to disease and attacks from the inhabitants. When Sir Francis Drake stopped by in 1586, the remaining men scrambled aboard his ships to return to England.

In 1587, another expedition led by John White made another attempt. A group of 117, including eighteen women (two of whom endured the harrowing voyage while pregnant) and nine children, set sail for Roanoke. On August 18, 1587, in Roanoke, Virginia Dare, White's granddaughter, became the first child of English parents born in America. No one expected the colony to be self-sufficient in the first years. Consequently, White returned to England almost immediately for new stores of provisions to keep the colony going.

By the time of his arrival, English spies had already brought word of a huge Spanish fleet of ships amassing for invasion. The execution of Mary, Queen of Scots, after a long imprisonment in the hands of her cousin, Elizabeth I, removed the last obstacle standing between Philip II of Spain and his ambitions for the English throne. While Protestant England was fair game for conquest in the eyes of Catholic Europe, Philip had no intention of mounting a campaign merely to put the Scottish queen, Elizabeth's rightful heir, in power. With Mary, viewed by many as a Catholic martyr, now dead, the way was clear for Philip to claim the throne for himself. His justification would be based on conquest, his nebulous tie as the husband of the previous English monarch, Mary (known to history as Bloody Mary), and as a Catholic rescuing England from the heresies of the New Learning.

The Spanish army, thousands of soldiers crammed into the holds of galleys, was considered unbeatable. Much like the military might of Nazi Germany against whom England stood alone in 1940, the Spanish army had defeated all who attempted to resist it. England's one hope in 1588 was her navy, their "wooden wall of defense." To that end, no ship could be spared, including the one carrying John White.

Not until March 1591, after the confirmed destruction of Philip's armada, did White return to Roanoke. He found the colony he had left deserted. That there was no sign of calamity provided some comfort: There were no graves or indications of battle. The colonists had evacuated but they clearly had had the time to make provision for their return, burying some of their belongings, doubtless to protect them from nearby Indian inhabitants. That they had been observed doing so was made evident in the open caches White found. More important, he also found a previously agreed signal that if the colonists had to leave, they would carve the name of where they had gone onto a post or tree. "Croatan" had been chiseled out in one spot and the letters CRO in another. There was a nearby island called Croatan as well as, in another location, an Indian people called Croatan.

White wanted to search for his missing family, but the captain of the ship on which he had sailed refused. His seaman's eye could spot the signs of a growing hurricane and he feared the shallow waters, quicksand, and other hazards of that coast-line, which would later earn it the name "Graveyard of the Atlantic." The only hope of safety for his ship was to reach open water as fast as possible. He never turned back. John White lived for fifteen more years, never learning the fate of his daughter, granddaughter, or the other hundred souls he had left on Roanoke Island. Thus the legend of the Lost Colony was born.

Modern Lumbee peoples living in eastern North Carolina lay claim to being descendents of these first English settlers, although few scholars give that assertion much credence. What happened to the Lost Colony remains one of the enduring mysteries of American history. At Breneau University in Gainesville, Georgia, there exists a collection of rocks known as the Dare Stones, proof of American fascination with the Lost Colony's fate.[1] The slabs all purport to contain messages carved by John White's daughter, Eleanor Dare. Most are obviously fraudulent, created and then presented by people for reasons best known to themselves. Two stones appear to be at least potentially authentic, perhaps left by Eleanor Dare. One says simply that her husband and daughter were dead; the second repeats that information, adding that the remaining colonists are on the run. Most likely the colonists had indeed taken refuge with the Croatan and were fleeing other Indian invaders.

Before disappearing into the mists of historical mystery, the first Roanoke settlers sent back to England specimens of the plant that would spur a subsequently successful colony, tobacco. Elizabeth I found it to be "intriguing." Her successor, James I, took another view, castigating the fumes as "harmful to the brain" and "dangerous to the lungs." Nonetheless, it was tobacco that would bring the next English venture on the North American continent to success.

The age of individual adventuring died on Tower Green when Sir Walter Ralegh lost his head, executed at the order of

James I. This first Stuart king, every bit as penny-pinching as his Tudor predecessors on whom he modeled himself, permitted English exploration to continue through the creation of joint-stock companies, thus minimizing Crown investment. This scheme also fostered colonial self-government. From the onset, English colonies stood in marked contrast to Spanish and French efforts that, especially in the case of the Spanish, were controlled in minute detail by the Crown.

In December 1606, the London Company launched three ships for America—the *Sarah Constant, Godspeed,* and *Discovery.* Commanded by Christopher Newport, this group of Englishmen landed on the south entrance to Chesapeake Bay, which they named Cape Henry in honor of the then Prince of Wales. The northern cape was named Charles after his brother, the Duke of York, the ill-fated Charles I, who was later executed on the balcony of St. James' Palace—the only English king to ever meet this fate.

They called the river leading inland the James, in honor of the king, and their settlement, Jamestowne, established on a defensible peninsula, the neck connecting it to the mainland so narrow as to render it almost an island. Seven councilors had been appointed by the king's charter; among them was John Smith.

The land chosen appeared most inviting to these men, weary after their voyage. Many accounts of this period include mention of the marvelous smells emanating from the dogwood and honeysuckle-filled forests as well as the rich strawberries, which were larger and sweeter than those they had known in England. But the spot soon proved treacherous as well. The first Jamestown settlers endured harsher climate swings—hotter summers and colder winters—than they had known in England. Worse, was the marshy setting with its accompanying mosquitoes carrying malaria and yellow fever. Nor were they welcomed by all of the Indian inhabitants of the region. Word had spread throughout the Indian nations of Spanish treatment of native peoples. Moreover, earlier Spanish attempts at incursion in the area had produced a justified wariness at yet another European invasion.

Fearing the threat posed by both the Spanish and nearby Indian peoples, the Jamestown settlers' first action was to build a fort, a palisade of tree trunks, on which they mounted canons at the triangular points of three bulwarks. Indeed, there were trees aplenty and it was those rich Virginia forests that first attracted the attention of these colonists in search of profit. Logs of oak and walnut filled the ships returning to England for fresh supplies. This walnut would soon become highly prized for English furniture making.

But disease, as well as Indian resistance, continued to take its toll. Admiral Newport returned on January 12, 1608, to find more than sixty of the original 104 settlers dead. Typhoid, unknowingly brought by one of the colonists, appeared to have been the principal culprit. Also, the winter of 1607–08, commonly known as the Great Frost, was one of the coldest ever recorded.

Still the colony persevered. Expeditions were sent out, ever determined to find the mythical Northwest Passage. Upon encountering the fall line near present-day Richmond, most turned back. Others simply disappeared. On one of these excursions, John Smith was taken captive. He eventually returned to the colony, the lone survivor of his party, later to create his tale (almost certainly exaggerated) of how Pocahontas, daughter of Chief Powhatan, had risked her life to save his.

In September 1608, Smith, despite the enmity he had fostered among many of the colonists, was made president of the council. He proceeded to inflict a rigid discipline that brought the colonists through yet another winter. The following year, Smith was badly injured when the powder on the boat in which he was asleep caught fire. He returned to England to

40

A tranquil aerial view of Jamestown Island.
CREDIT: Virginia Historical Society

recover. While recuperating, he wrote his famous memoirs—the account of Pocahontas saving his life appears in the last revision.[2] This scene of Powhatan's daughter running to place her head over Smith's even as the club had been raised to execute him has long been the stuff of legend, retold in many accounts and captured often on canvas. The most famous painting is probably French artist Victor Nehlig's 1870 *Pocahontas and John Smith*, exhibited at the 1893 World's Columbian Exposition in Chicago.

The years of 1609 and 1610 brought the worst experience the colonists had yet encountered—the Starving Time. Of the approximately five hundred men, women, and children present in the colony in late 1609, only sixty were still alive the following spring.

Although disease continued to be a problem, the hunger and malnutrition that had threatened the survival of Jamestown began to abate as the colonists learned to cultivate indigenous vegetables. A 1613 report refers to Indian corn, Indian peas, and Indian beans. From native peoples, the colonists also learned to utilize the soil replenishing techniques of crop rotation—wheat one year, followed by grass, followed by corn.

But the permanence of the colony was assured by John Rolfe, who developed a milder, less biting tobacco and then devised a process of curing it to survive the salty air it would encounter during its shipment to England. In 1614, Rolfe married the captive Pocahontas, although not until she converted to Christianity, accepting baptism as Rebecca. He even took his new wife and their young son to England, where Pocahontas was treated as visiting royalty, evidence of English misperceptions of the Indian peoples whose land they had ventured upon. Unfortunately, Pocahontas did not survive the journey. She died in March 1617 as they began the voyage back to America and was interred at St. George's Chapel in Gravesend, the first American Indian to be buried by the banks of the Thames. The whereabouts of her grave is indeterminable today as a result of German Luftwaffe bombing of the East End during World War II.

The union of one of the Virginia Colony's leaders and Powhatan's daughter brought an eight-year period of peace to the settlement. The colony also prospered under the stern but effective leadership of Sir Thomas Dale. In 1611, Dale found a healthier site for the settlement, upriver on Farrar's Island, at a site he named Henrico for Henry, Prince of Wales. Dale imposed strict government on the colony, including harsh penalties for shirkers. Indeed, his *Lawes Divine, Morall and Martiall* detailed a long list of offenses along with ruthless consequences for anyone caught breaking those laws (including burnings at the stake).[3]

Equally important, Dale put an end to the communal sharing of labor and its rewards under which Jamestown had operated since its founding, opting instead to prompt labor through the profits of private property. The headright system was created to offer fifty acres of land to any man willing to pay for his own passage to the Jamestown colony. In addition, he received an additional fifty acres for each member of his family and each servant who traveled with him. Puritan settlers in Massachusetts Bay would scorn this rewarding of land to those who brought servants, but those men were precisely the sort of settlers Virginia wanted—men of property who arrived to find still more riches in the New World.

The combined incentive of free land plus the proven profitability of tobacco cultivation brought increased immigration to the Virginia Colony. Settling both banks of the James River, they moved inland quickly, pushing aside native peoples. In 1622, Opechancanough, who assumed leadership of the Powhatan Confederacy, struck back.

On Good Friday morning, March 22, the well-coordinated attack began on both sides of the river from the Hampton Roads area all the way to the falls. Over 350 colonists perished, including John Rolfe. Retaliation that fall and winter was merciless, breaking the back of the once powerful confederacy. Opechancanough would wait until 1644 before mounting another effort at resistance, that time doomed to failure.

One by one, all of the tribes living in Virginia were moved off their lands, most of them several times, relocated first to one spot and then forced to move on as the British colony grew. A few, friendly to the English, were allowed to remain on severely diminished land holdings. Most were pushed to reservations farther to the west, establishing a pattern than would be repeated throughout American history—the creation of reserves for Indian peoples on land no farmer would want, always to the west of their own established settlements.

Notes

1. Thanks are owed to Brenau University for providing information and access to this collection. For more information, contact them at One Centennial Circle, Gainesville, GA 30501.
2. John Smith, *The generall historie of Virginia, New England and the Summer Isles, together with The true travels, adventures and observations, and A sea grammar, by Captaine John Smith* (Glasgow: J. MacLehose, 1907).
3. Virginius Dabney, *Virginia, The New Dominion* (New York: Doubleday and Company, Inc., 1971), pp. 24–29.

Chapter Four
Self-Rule

An important date of ironic contrasts in Virginia history is 1619. That year the first non-Indian representative Assembly in the New World met—the Virginia General Assembly. Spearheaded by Sir Edwin Sandys, head of the London Company, the House of Burgesses was elected by all freemen in the colony, including indentured servants, thus marking the start of the democratic experiment that would later produce the United States. But 1619 also saw the arrival of the first Dutch ships bringing Africans to Virginia. Ostensibly indentured servants, these new laborers were marked as different from the start, although slave codes would not be introduced into law for decades. The demand for labor to work the tobacco fields was overwhelming: by 1630, the colony produced a million pounds of tobacco annually. Approximately four thousand blacks were brought to Virginia during the second half of the seventeenth century, with over half of those arrivals between 1675 and 1700, and the majority in the last decade—testimony to the profit to be gained through tobacco and the willingness of the English colonists to adopt slavery to achieve it.

The new charter of 1618 and the establishment of "particulars," or private plantations, increased population dispersion, making any central administration difficult. Virginia was first divided into four particulars—James City, Henrico City, Charles City, and Elizabeth City. Thirty-two elected Burgesses from these plantations plus a Governor's Council of six chosen by the London Company made up the Assembly.[1]

Local councils were organized on each plantation and a commander appointed to deal with the ever-present threat of Indian resistance along with a continuing fear of Spanish attack. Monthly courts, originating in 1622, moved around the settlements to deal with disputes (principally concerning land). By 1629, the monthly courts began appointing officers to serve as keepers of the peace, rather like their constable counterparts in the Mother Country. Within three years, five monthly courts were established; Virginia was well on its way to the creation of county government.

The decentralization process remained steady. In 1634, the House of Burgesses created eight counties. Various powers were split between the county courts, the Assembly, and the governor. But the counties assumed more and more power. By the middle of the seventeenth century, most issues that touched peoples' daily lives were taken care of at the county level.

The county courts consisted of justices of the peace, a sheriff, a clerk, and various deputies. Determined to retain their identity as Englishmen, forever fearing that the wilderness in which they now found themselves would change them, separating them from their countrymen on the other side of the Atlantic, the Virginia colonists deliberately chose the titles and assigned the various office responsibilities almost precisely as they would have been in any English county. The sheriff policed the area and, as a new duty, collected taxes. Originally, the governor selected the sheriff, but the justices of the peace soon assumed the process. By the 1660s, they were rotating the office among themselves.

These justices of the peace tended to be self-perpetuating. When one died, the remaining justices nominated someone to take his place. In actuality, they controlled the political process on the county level—an entrenched local elite.

As time went on, the county court took over the powers belonging to the vestries in England. Societal development follows as a consequence of economic realities—in Virginia, that meant a rural populace, widely dispersed, with each family garnering as much land as possible for tobacco cultivation. A rapidly growing population spreading out far from each other weakened the strength of the Anglican Church over the colony. County courts filled that power void, assuming autonomy over day-to-day affairs, a stance that often placed them in conflict with the governor and the Assembly.

The fourth charter granted to the London Company in 1618 to organize the House of Burgesses intended to bring the representatives of the various plantations together with the company to resolve their conflicts. The Burgesses met annually until 1624, when Virginia became a royal colony. But England's efforts to bring new organization to the colony failed to slow the growing trend toward self-government.

As a royal colony, three principal bodies ruled Virginia. The chief office was that of governor, first appointed in 1625. His duties were to act as the king's surrogate, enforcing royal policies, appointing lesser officials, and acting as the final court of appeal in the judicial system. More importantly, he dispensed patronage and allocated land. He also controlled meetings of the Assembly, calling them into session, and retained the right of veto. Interestingly, the writ and instructions prepared by the Crown for each governor appointed never changed in the years that followed despite developments in the Virginia colony. By the end of the seventeenth century, the House of Burgesses had emasculated the governor's office, often nominating one of their own elite to serve in the office. Yet the Crown's instructions never wavered, often putting the governor, usually a Virginia property owner, in a difficult position, forcing him to make decisions that would result in either his recall or a rebellion among his neighbors.

The second ruling body was the Council. By law, the Crown could appoint a new council whenever the governor changed or a new monarch came to the throne. But in practice, the councilors remained the same, eventually becoming a self-perpetuating oligarchy. This, not the governor's office, was the seat of true power; soon the goal of all ambitious Virginians was to secure a seat on the Council. Originally, it was formed to advise the governor, legislate, and dispense justice, but the Council quickly became a sort of upper house of the Assembly with the House of Burgesses acting as the lower house. The creation of the county courts in 1634 relieved the Council of a great deal of its judicial burden so they could concentrate instead on making decisions about land claims. This was the Council's true power and the reason why already wealthy Virginia colonists sought seats on the body.

From 1624 until 1634, the House of Burgesses met only three times, but after 1639, they met annually. From the onset, they struggled to wrest power from the Council, succeeding in establishing procedures for their election and the basis of representation. Although the Burgesses' prestige grew, it was still difficult to convince busy farmers to take time away from their fields to meet. Finding four men willing to travel for their Assembly duties became difficult, so in 1660, the Burgesses reduced the representatives to two men from each county, mandating that the county must pay salaries to their representatives. In 1669, they added a further incentive, voting to penalize those counties that did not send two representatives.

The central importance of this process to Virginia, indeed all of subsequent American political development, was that representation was tied to the counties. In England during this same period, virtual representation was becoming the norm. But in Virginia, actual representation; that is, that a man must reside in the county he represented, evolved as law.

Moreover, the Burgesses' power continued to grow, marked by their ability to elect their own officers. Their Speaker was not appointed by the governor; a marked contrast to the Crown's appointment of the Speaker of the House of Commons. Most importantly, they assumed the right to initiate legislation, which was particularly necessary in two crucial areas—the collection of taxes and the establishment of a budget. Controlling the purse strings gave them enormous sway in the government of the colony.

The onset of civil war in England and the period of Interregnum, which followed between 1649 and 1660, affected the New England colonies more than they did Virginia. Fiercely loyal to the throne, Virginia's governor, Sir William Berkeley, encouraged those "Cavaliers" who had supported the ill-fated Charles I to emigrate to America. Some did, including the first Carters, Lees, Masons, and Randolphs, families who would become leaders of the Commonwealth. Those years were marked by continued tobacco development and the resulting struggle for political control over the land and the economy.

In reality, no one had control over the economy. The continual fluctuation in tobacco prices created an unstable financial system. The primary problem lay in overproduction. By 1700, the Chesapeake area produced 38 million pounds of tobacco a year. Equally challenging was the issue of marketing.

By 1650, Virginians had fallen prey to a consignment system; that is, they sold tobacco through English merchants who paid all of the marketing costs in exchange for a percentage of profits. Merchants advanced goods to the planters in trade for the coming year's crop, so planters were continually in hock to those merchants. As a result, demand had nothing to do with how much tobacco was grown. Planters continually cultivated more and more to try to pay off their debts.

Another problem lay in Virginia's attempts to expand into European markets. Because they were an English colony, Virginians were legally required to ship all tobacco through England. But England could not absorb more than one-third of the crop. Demand existed throughout Europe for superior Virginia tobacco. Some countries tried to keep out American tobacco by banning or taxing it, finally farming out monopolies.

The instability of an economy based almost solely on tobacco had profound social consequences. The demand for more land put pressure on Indian peoples, sometimes necessitating military action to fulfill the Virginia's thirst for new soil. Moreover, the ever-growing tobacco fields produced a great demand for labor. Indentured servants and free labor couldn't fill that need; neither system worked consistently in any case. What incentive existed for one man to work for another when he could simply move farther west and obtain his own land? After 1670, blacks were relied upon as a chief source of labor. Increased tobacco production cemented the slave system in the South. Between 1680 and 1720, over forty thousand slaves were brought into Virginia alone (the numbers grew substantially when Maryland and other Southern colonies are included).

Finally, an economy based on the concept of cash crop shaped Southern societal development. The wide, deep, and, most favorably, westward flowing rivers of the South enabled populations to spread quickly into the interior. In marked contrast to the North, the South had no need for urban centers and consequently developed none.

Virginia's difficulties produced by its continual tobacco surplus only intensified after 1660 with the Restoration in England. The new king, Charles II, needed money to maintain the ostentatious court with which he surrounded himself. The Navigation Act of 1660 aggravated the colony's already shaky economy by reinforcing previous restrictions that all American tobacco be shipped to England. In reaction, Virginians experimented briefly with other crops. These attempts at diversification proved unsuccessful because nothing grew as well in Virginia as tobacco did. Besides, the planters already had so much invested in tobacco that they were loath to abandon the crop. The English Crown, also dependent on those tobacco revenues, put pressure on Virginians to continue tobacco production.

Other problems exacerbated the growing fear of Virginians that their colony was in decline. There existed considerable tension between the colonists at large and Governor William

Berkeley, who was widely, and probably correctly, perceived as a stooge of the large tobacco planters. Terrible crops in the early 1670s brought on by droughts and a work force downed by epidemics coincided with the Second War with the Dutch. Parliament showed little sympathy, passing more navigation legislation. The Plantation Act of 1673 cut off Virginia from New England where the colony had previously gotten a good deal of its food, thereby freeing fields that might have been allocated to growing foodstuffs for tobacco cultivation.

Worst of all, the new king, Charles II, began asserting his ability to make land grants in those New World areas claimed by the English. Most famous was his gift of all the land between the southern edge of Virginia and the northern rim of Spanish Florida to eight men, known as proprietors, resulting in the creation of the Carolina colony.[2] Charles I had made similar grants in Virginia in the 1640s. In the 1670s, those earlier proprietors began claiming quitrents and the right to establish manorial courts. Their numbers grew as Charles II granted almost all of the rest of Virginia, much of it already settled by Englishmen, to a new group of proprietors who proposed to do the same thing.

Virginia's solution to this challenge to their already shaky commercial well-being was to approach the king to buy out those proprietors. While they were at it, the first colonists tried to secure their future rights to property. The Virginia General Assembly sent three agents to England, to ask for a new charter that would secure the claims of those English Virginians already in place along with a royal promise not to give away their lands. Moreover, they demanded that all judicial trials (almost all of which concerned land disputes) be held in Virginia. They also wanted the power of the Assembly confirmed, most especially a guarantee that there would be no taxes levied in Virginia except those approved by the governor, Council, and Burgesses. In essence, they were demanding their rights as Englishmen, local political autonomy; that is, no taxation without representation.

The Lords of Trade, organized in 1675, at first approved the charter but later opposed it, urging the king not to sign, arguing that this agreement would make Virginia too independent and did nothing to help England regulate Virginia's tobacco trade. Most crucially, news of Bacon's Rebellion reached England, effectively squashing all efforts to secure the desired charter in 1676.

Conflict with Indian peoples had never truly disappeared as an ever-present danger to all Virginians—white, red, and black. But intermittent skirmishes erupted into new war in 1675. By the time the General Assembly met in the following March, nearly three hundred colonists had been killed.[3] Governor Berkeley refused to retaliate with military action, prompting thirty-eight-year-old Nathaniel Bacon, Jr., to organize an expedition. Although a member of Council himself, Bacon drew most of his followers from backwoodsmen, westerners who put little faith in the colony's eastern leaders, those rich tobacco planters along the James River, to protect them. The first victims were a group of Occaneechee, on an island in the Roanoke River, slaughtered by Bacon's men in May 1676.

Charged with treason, Bacon was brought before the governor. Now elderly and possessing what was reputed to be a filthy temper, William Berkeley could still sense how the wind was blowing among the colonists who had adopted Bacon as a popular hero. In return for Bacon's petition for pardon, Berkeley granted it, restoring Bacon to the Council and promising to give him a commission to fight Indians. But the middle class and backwoodsmen of Virginia had acquired a taste for power. In the 1676 elections, an overwhelming number of Baconians as they now called themselves, including a number of leading planters, were elected Burgesses. When Berkeley's promised commission never materialized, Bacon took action.

On June 23, he led more than a hundred armed followers to Jamestown, surrounding the statehouse, forcing the governor to grant that commission. But the Baconians went further, forcing a number of concessions, including a pardon for their "treason." Significantly, during the final days of the Assembly's session, new statutes—Bacon's Laws—were enacted, which did much to break the control of the rich planters' oligarchy and further democracy in the colony. The ballot was now extended to all freemen, enabling them to elect representatives who would have control over taxes levied and local ordinances passed.

Berkeley went along with the Assembly while Bacon's army was still in Jamestown. As soon as they left, he declared them rebels and ordered a force to be organized to march against them. But while Berkeley found little support for his summons among the county militiamen, Bacon quickly put together a group of some thirteen hundred men, forcing Berkeley to flee across the Chesapeake Bay to Accomack while Bacon's men took possession of the mainland, making his headquarters at Middle Plantation, the site of present-day Williamsburg. A true civil war was now underway. Even Jamestown was burned in the conflicts that followed between the governor's forces and Bacon's better-organized men.

The ceaseless fighting took its toll on people as well as structures. Bacon was one of the victims, falling ill to dysentery and dying in October. Without their charismatic leader, Bacon's army fell apart, its leaders hunted down and hanged by Berkeley who was determined to have his revenge.

This uproar did little to convince Parliament or the Crown that Virginia could govern itself. A new charter was granted in 1676, giving the colonists control over their lands, but the requested legislative autonomy for the Assembly was denied. No attention was paid to the Burgesses' demand for their own consent to all taxation.

Charles II had already ordered a military expedition sent to the colony to defeat the Indian peoples and protect Berkeley, whom the king scorned. Rather his goal was to remove the

Indian threat that had given rise to Bacon's Rebellion, hoping to eliminate future outbreaks of trouble. Eleven hundred troops in eight ships set sail to assert imperial control. Their leader, Colonial Hubert Jeffries, replaced Berkeley as governor. The latter was exiled back to England while Jeffries expelled the Council and forced the Burgesses to accept laws written in England.

Like so many others, Jeffries soon died as a result of disease contracted in Virginia. He was replaced by Thomas Lord Culpeper, who arrived in 1680, determined to negotiate a settlement that would allow the army to return home, thereby saving considerable royal expenditure. The result was the Imperial Compromise, voluntarily passed by the Assembly, guaranteeing the Crown a fixed annual revenue to be submitted by the Virginia colony. Charles II won what he most wanted—steady profit that was not reliant upon fluctuating tobacco prices. But Virginia won also in Culpeper's agreement not to enforce the Crown's attempted inroads on local autonomy.

Commercial, not political, concerns motivated the Virginia Assembly. With peace restored, they looked to their fields, continuing to plant tobacco. But the principles raised in Bacon's Rebellion and the demands of the Burgesses for a new charter in 1675 were not forgotten. No taxation without representation would become the rallying cry for another revolution a hundred years later.

Notes

1. The word "Burgess" was adopted from the English term denoting borough representatives.
2. *Carol*, Latin for Charles, provided the colony's name.
3. Virginius Dabney, *Virginia: The New Dominion* (New York: Doubleday and Company, 1971), 58.

Chapter Five
Are We Englishmen?

Contrary to popular myth and aspiration, America never existed as a classless society. Englishmen immigrating to North America sought to recreate the social structures they had known at home. Nowhere was oligarchic rule more firmly entrenched than in Virginia, in part as a result of the number of "Cavaliers" who arrived in the colony during the English civil wars and following Charles I's execution in 1649. Accustomed to power and prestige, they rose quickly to leadership in the colony.

But in Virginia, it was land, not title, which marked the ruling class. Some one hundred families made up the colony's elite, a small group determined to maintain and, when possible, expand their influence, largely through intermarriage with one another. These were marriages made to secure land mergers, often with unhappy results. Still, the wealth was maintained. From a single marriage between William Randolph and Mary Isham, many of Virginia's future leadership descended included, John Marshall, Thomas Jefferson, Robert E. Lee, and Edmund Randolph among the most famous.[1] Another example of this intermarriage between families can be found in the case of George Washington's nephew Major Lawrence Lewis who in 1799 married Martha Washington's granddaughter from her previous marriage, Nelly Custis. To celebrate their wedding, Washington presented the young couple with two thousand acres of his Mount Vernon estate for the construction of their magnificent home, Woodlawn, which may still be visited in Alexandria today.[2]

The tobacco-planter class built stately homes for themselves. Slave labor enabled them to afford such luxuries, and freed them to pursue social prominence and even leisure time for games. Tenpins, a sort of lawn bowling game, was popular, as were all forms of gambling, most especially on horse racing. From the beginning, Virginia was horse country.

A strong middle class grew as well, incorporating men who rose from humble origins to secure land in the Virginia colony. The strength of their numbers was evident in the rapid response of men willing to fight whenever Bacon summoned them. Some even aspired to join—and thus acquire the prerogatives of—the ruling class.

Social status was most readily apparent through clothing. Gentlemen wore lace collars and doublets, and sported elaborate headwear and silver-buckled shoes. Even the swords belted to their waists were accoutrements of the upper class. Their wives' attire consisted of silk gowns, hoop skirts topped by bodices of satin or linen. Lace-trimmed bonnets and fans completed the women's opulent attire, along with jewelry of diamonds and/or pearls.

The upper and middle classes alike enjoyed an ample food source. Venison was commonly found on most tables, along with turkey and fish. All farms, rich or poor, raised cattle, chickens, sheep, and hogs. In many ways, the diet of Virginians was far superior to that of Englishmen still on the other side of the Atlantic. The vegetables that the Indian peoples had taught the Jamestown colonists to grow were perpetuated by later colonists. The forests provided rich sources of berries as well as walnuts, chestnuts, and pecans, put to good use in devising famous Southern delicacies of pecan pie and black walnut cake.

Still, the emerging aristocracy in Virginia, despite their efforts to copy every detail of fashion and deportment common

among their counterparts still in England, remained funda-
mentally different. First and foremost, they recognized no
common interests among themselves. Rather, every man acted
in self-interest (witness those planters who joined Bacon's
forces against Berkeley). Second, only wealth, not education
nor ancestry, distinguished these people. Third, they never
enjoyed any sense of security. Prominence achieved by wealth
could be lost quickly, either through storms or pirates eliminating a year's crop, or through a loss of political patronage.

The most striking dissimilarity between the aristocracy of
Virginia and that of the Mother Country was the continual
presence of slavery, a blot on American history for which all
English colonists, North and South, must share blame. In the
late seventeenth century, for example, 35 to 40 percent of
Boston men claimed to own shares in a slave ship. Research
among the shipping records of the seventeenth and eighteenth
centuries reveals the names of the most prominent men in the
colonies as investors, many of whose holdings included, at
least in part, slave trafficking.

From the outset, Virginians looked upon blacks as inferior
people, a consequence of the cultural baggage they had
brought with them as Englishmen. During a century of rising
nationalism, English explorers in the 1500s had scorned
Africans for their lack of political organization. The land of
Shakespeare recognized no culture among the Africans. Moreover, their very color invoked negative images in English
minds. Black was the color of disease (the Black Death), witch-
craft, and a sign of God's curse; some tracts of that age suggest
that blacks were descendants of Ham, marked by God in punishment for Ham "looking upon Noah's nakedness." Like the
American Indian, the Africans were not Christian, and therefore were viewed by Europeans as pagan—deserving of whatever fate befell them.

Still, slavery, perpetual servitude that could be inherited, never existed in England. Those first twenty blacks arriving in the Virginia colony in 1619 did not come as slaves, but the increasing demand for a permanent work force prompted a descent into servitude in the decades that followed. In the 1630s, black indentured laborers were being sold for much higher prices than their white counterparts, a good indicator that their terms of service were for far longer. Tax rolls at the time contain the names of black women, evidence that they were being used for fieldwork; white female servants were not. A case in 1639 further illuminates the growth of slavery in practice if not actually in law. A white servant who had run away was sentenced by the court to a doubling of his time of indentured servitude. A black servant was given thirty lashes; evidence that his time of service was already so lengthy that there could be no point in doubling it.

In 1660, Virginia made slavery official by law. Still, there were not yet a thousand blacks in the colony. White indentured servants still undertook most of the labor. Here again, Bacon's Rebellion proved to be a watershed event. Most of his foot soldiers were former indentured servants who had sought land on the frontier and were therefore most in danger of attack by Indian peoples. Many Eastern Virginia planters decided to stop bringing in indentured servants and the slave imports increased substantially. By 1700, the black population in Virginia stood at six thousand, almost all bought from the West Indies, where slavery was murderously harsh, so horrendous that only the strongest had any chance of survival.

As a consequence of the need for field labor, the ratio of male to female slaves remained two to one throughout the seventeenth century. The vast majority of slave-owners only possessed two or three people. This dispersion made marriage among slaves practically impossible. It was not until the eighteenth century that African-American cultural foundations could be laid, as larger numbers of slaves made it possible for blacks to begin families. By the middle of the century, Virginians were encouraging those unions, to perpetuate their labor force. As tobacco prices continued to spiral downward, Virginia colonists sought to acquire more land, requiring more labor, necessitating increasing numbers of slaves.

Black or white, all Virginians fought disease, the prevalence of which was a further factor separating Englishmen in the New World from their fellow countrymen at home. Between 1607 and 1624, less than one in six of those immigrating to Virginia survived. The mortality figures improved in the decades that followed, but European diseases combined with new American maladies—malaria and yellow fever chief among them—continued to make Virginia a dangerous place to live. In 1699, the colony's capital was moved from Jamestown to the healthier ground of Middle Plantation, renamed Williamsburg in honor of the king, William III who, with his wife Mary, daughter of James II, had come to the throne in 1689.

Still, the average life expectancy in the Southern colonies was ten years less than that recorded among populations in England for the same period. By contrast, Englishmen settling in New England, both men and women, possessed an average life expectancy of seventy-one and seventy respectively, some twenty years longer than Virginia colonists. This disparity reflects not only the disease spread by Southern mosquitoes, but also patterns of settlement. The Massachusetts Bay colony and its offshoots in Connecticut and Rhode Island relocated in groups, almost always around a church. In town, help was more readily found when accidents occurred. In Virginia, a lone farmer whose ax slipped as he was attempting to clear his land bled to death, too far from assistance.

These population statistics can be misleading. That the average life expectancy for a woman in the Virginia colony was fifty must be viewed in the context of the large numbers of young women who died in childbirth. Those women who survived their child-bearing years had a good chance of living well into their eighties or even their nineties. These widows, sometimes in possession of considerable property, were highly sought after as marriage prospects, often by far younger men, to the consternation of young Virginia women who feared spinsterhood. One of the more colorful examples of this practice can be found in a wedding announcement printed in the *Virginia Gazette* in 1771 describing the nuptials of a twenty-three-year-old man to Sarah Ellyson, a widow, eight-five years old, but "a sprightly old Tit with three thousand pounds fortune."

All of the English colonists stretched out along the Atlantic seaboard were aware of their growing provincialism. For the most part, New Englanders appear to have accepted their new identity as Americans. They were still Englishmen, of course, but a new breed, far more concerned about their homes and local concerns than any political or social developments happening in the mother country. By contrast, Virginians, many of whom fancied themselves more closely tied to English aristocracy, were particularly concerned by the perceptible differences between themselves and the nobility of England.

One example is William Byrd II. He spent twenty-five years building Westover Plantation, copied in every detail from an estate in England. He also fancied himself an author, writing *History of the Dividing Line*. Interestingly, he published two versions of his book, one written in earthy terms, criticizing his fellow Virginia landowners. That copy was intended for sale in America. A second, authored with a careful eye to copying a style of prose then popular in England, eliminates that critique, opting instead to underscore the similarities between English and Virginia gentlemen.

But this second book, intended for an English audience, did not sell well there. In fact, few Englishmen gave much thought

The main house of Westover Plantation, one of the many "houses that tobacco built."
CREDIT: H. Harry Bagby, Virginia Historical Society

to the colonies at all as the seventeenth century came to an end. Both Crown and Parliament were aware of the growing disparity as well, but cared only that Virginia continue to be a source of profit. The Glorious Revolution in 1688–89 brought William and Mary to the throne and established a Protestant religious settlement once and for all through the Bill of Rights. It was hailed by the American colonists whose publications made it clear that they failed to understand the basic power shift that had occurred. It was Parliament, not the Crown, which now chiefly ruled.

61

After 1800, fewer Englishmen immigrated to America. Most new arrivals came from Africa. Almost four thousand Scotch-Irish emigrated annually from Ulster to America, many of them settling in the mountain areas of the South, including Virginia. From these new arrivals, the traditions of Virginia's mountain communities sprang, adding new words to the dialect—sparkin' for courting, critter for creature, young'un for child, and so forth. Fiddle music provided the entertainment, bringing the songs of Scotland and Ireland to America, giving the songs a distinctive Southern sound.

Free land attracted these new immigrants as much as it had their English predecessors a century before. In 1705, Virginia abandoned headrights in favor of land warrants. Under this new system, a man could get as much property as he wanted and could work. Similar systems were devised in Maryland and North Carolina, almost all for tobacco cultivation. Between 1745 and 1760, there was a sharp increase in immigration to the English colonies in America.

Per capita income during this period increased 3 percent per year, a development spawned in part by improved agricultural techniques. More importantly, in Britain the price of manufactured goods remained stable and the demand for colonial exports went up, particularly for lumber and tobacco, both of which Virginia could supply. This proven profitability led to a competition among British merchants for American investment. The transatlantic economy, which had been the principal reason for establishing the Virginia colony, was finally working. But Virginians remained second-class citizens in the eyes of the British who still lived in England; the colonists were people to whom the British gave little thought. For their part, Virginians who could afford it continued to ape the manners and abodes of an aristocracy with whom they had little enough in common.

Notes

1. Virginius Dabney, *Virginia: The New Dominion* (New York: Doubleday and Company, 1971), 47.
2. To view Woodlawn Plantation, please visit the following Web site: www.virginia.org and click on "historic homes."

Chapter Six
"Give Me Liberty . . ."

The 1689 settlement in England had put several limits on the Crown's prerogatives. Parliamentary legislation was required for the Crown to create new courts; the king could not dismiss judges. No taxes were permitted without a parliamentary grant. Royal standing armies were prohibited; the Crown could raise an army during war only with parliamentary approval. The king or queen could not interfere in any way with Parliament; indeed, in 1707 the last royal veto was cast.

In the colonies, things were far different, underscoring for the colonials their diminished standing within the British Empire. Here, governors had and used veto power. Any law signed by the governor could still be turned down by the Privy Council or the king. Colonial governors could prorogue assemblies at their whim or they could hold an assembly as long as they liked, trapping plantation owners in the capitol while they passed the legislation that the royal government demanded. On the other side of the coin, governors could refuse to call the assembly into session, a tactic the irascible Governor Berkeley often employed. Judges were dependent on the royal governors who could create courts.

In practice, informal compromises on both sides of the Atlantic ameliorated the sharper aspects of those laws. Colonial assemblies paid the governor's salary. Moreover, he was usually native to the colony and not anxious to act against his own as well as his neighbors' best interests. Still, orders came from London, often forcing governors to introduce unpopular legislation, raising the ire of colonial assemblies, whose members chafed under the yoke of what they perceived to be an uncaring and disinterested Parliament.

Virginia was a singularly harmonious exception to the increasing animosity that grew throughout the colonies in the eighteenth century. This was the only colony that achieved a working cooperation between all branches of government. Virginia's entrenched social system made this possible. Its citizens looked up to the planters as their political leaders, content to let them rule while the average man concentrated on his own farm and the livelihood of his family. There were no quarrels over religion in Virginia, in marked contrast to New England. Finally, the economy continued to be dominated by tobacco production, unlike in other English colonies—Massachusetts and New York, for example—where large merchant classes existed. A great deal of unity based on common interest held Virginians together.

The colony also benefited from wise political leadership during the first half of the eighteenth century. Governor Spotswood realized he must work with the Virginia gentry and did his best to act as a buffer between English demands and planter aspirations. Governor John Gouch (1727–49) followed this same practice. A pragmatic and judicious man, he sought compromise continually. Widely recognized and respected for his scrupulous honesty, he always had a working majority in the House of Burgesses, no small help in keeping the peace. Yet ironically, the catalyst for the American Revolution was a conflict that began in Virginia—the French and Indian.

In a period sometimes known as the Second Hundred Years' War, the British and the French engaged in a series of intermittent conflicts beginning in the last decade of the seventeenth century with King William's War. There followed Queen Anne's War and then King George's War in the first half of the eighteenth century. While some skirmishes took place in North America, primarily between Indian peoples fighting for their respective European allies, these first three wars were fought, for the most part, on the Continent. The fourth, however, known in Europe as the Seven Years' War, had a far greater impact on the colonies. It continued for two years after Great Britain and the French had negotiated a peace, because Indian peoples refused to surrender. To Americans, this was the French and Indian War.

Concerned about growing English populations along the Atlantic seaboard, which were beginning to push beyond the Appalachian Mountains, the French dispatched armed expeditions into the Ohio River Valley in 1752. There they built forts, a military barrier linking Canada to Louisiana.

Of course, a number of Virginia land companies also laid claim to the Ohio River Valley. In 1754, Governor Robert Dinwiddie sent a militia group, commanded by George Washington, to survey and report on the French military presence. Engaging the French in battle, Washington's group was soundly beaten and sent scurrying back to Virginia, which promptly notified London of the French "attack." Britain responded by declaring war once again on the French. They sent two military regiments to Virginia and called for a combined colonial force to be made up of volunteers.

The first years of the war proved disastrous for the British and their colonial allies. Overconfident of their success and expecting to fight the war cheaply, Great Britain undersupplied the colonies and sent incompetent leadership as well. The colonial militias were drilled to march in formation and fight a European infantry–style war in which opposing forces lined up to meet in open field combat. Indian peoples did not intend to fight that way, a reality the Virginians knew well enough. General Edward Braddock's defeat and the loss of half of his troops in 1755 proved the Virginians right.

When William Pitt became prime minister in late 1756, he resolved to take all French possessions. Now willing to properly supply the colonists, the British appointed adequate officers, but the war had already strained relations with their American colonies. Colonial soldiers, in particular, viewed the British with disdain. Approximately five thousand men had volunteered at the onset of the conflict—a remarkable outpouring, motivated as always by self-interest. They were frontiersmen for the most part, hoping to push Indian peoples away from their lands. But after 1756, the British were forced to turn to conscription and impressments to fill their ranks. They began seizing whatever was needed to supply the troops from colonial merchants and farmers as well. Despite colonial objections, the British brought in the press gangs whose tactics were viewed as outright kidnapping by the colonials whose sons were taken. Additionally, the colonists did not appreciate British schemes to lure their apprentices and other workers away. Colonial labor, always in short supply, was needed elsewhere.

Until 1756, the colonists and the British fought under their own commanders. Their units ordered combined in that year, the colonials resented their loss of rank in the British army. They also objected to the harsh code of military conduct, with its swift, often brutal, punishments, commonplace under British law. The primary difference between the two groups is that while the colonial soldiers were, for the most part, middle-class farmers, joined by some artisans and unskilled laborers in the northern colonies, British regular soldiers were made up of what Americans viewed as the scum of society. Harsh penalties were necessary to shape those men, pressed into service from among the dregs of British cities, into a fighting force. Frankly, Americans did not want their sons associating with that sort of riffraff.

British army officers, generally well born, professional, and older than their colonial counterparts, viewed the colonial militia officers as social upstarts and inexperienced amateurs.

For their part, the colonial officers felt they, not the British, possessed far better knowledge of how to pursue a wilderness campaign, a fact they thought had been made clear by Braddock's defeat. But the British refused to relinquish one iota of authority and went further, restricting colonial trade and, beginning in 1760, issuing Writs of Assistance, authorizing British military officials to inspect all colonial ships and warehouses, confiscating whatever property they wished.

The British had Indian allies as well, although far fewer than the French. In the North, most of the Iroquois Confederacy either chose or were coerced into fighting for the British. In the South, the Cherokee allied themselves with the British to fight their enemy tribes. However, the majority of Indian peoples chose to fight for the French. The British began paying bounties for Indian scalps, a policy decision that backfired terribly. In the Shenandoah Valley in 1760, a group of bounty hunters attacked a party of Cherokee, killing and scalping them, leaving their bodies to rot where they had fallen. This turned the tide of the war in Virginia as many Cherokee now joined those Indian people brought together by a forceful Ottawa leader, Pontiac. It was Pontiac who formed the first pan-Indian military force in American history, as tribes put aside their age-old enmities to fight the common menace of continued English expansion.

The French surrendered in 1761, defeated in Europe by British forces. But the French and Indian War in America continued. Those colonists who had already poured over the Appalachian Mountains following Daniel Boone and others to settle portions of what is now known as Kentucky and Tennessee were forced to fall back. The western Virginia frontier ran with blood. In the end, Britain negotiated a truce with Pontiac, the key element of which was a line to be drawn down the Appalachian Mountains, designating all territory to the west to be closed to English settlement and reserved for Indian peoples. This Proclamation of 1763 outraged the colonists, who had fought the war to gain those lands.

The French and Indian War marks a dividing point in Virginia history. Indeed, throughout the thirteen British colonies, people expressed their anger at perceived British incompetence in fighting the war; Parliamentary negligence in dealing with colonial concerns, abuses the British forces had inflicted on colonial populations, and most importantly the new law prohibiting settlement. It was a Virginian, Patrick Henry, a young man with an incredible talent for oratory, who first referred to the British king as a "tyrant" who "forfeits all rights to his subject's obedience."

Ignoring colonial protests, the British proceeded to pass a series of tax acts in an effort to replenish a severely depleted treasury after nearly a century of intermittent wars with the French. Most ignominious of these new laws was the Stamp Act. This tax was imposed on all handwritten documents and printed papers alike—from marriage licenses, to wills, to newspapers, and even playing cards. It was also the first legislation not disguised as some sort of trade regulation. Rather, the Stamp Act was a naked scheme to make money for the Mother Country.

Patrick Henry led the fight against the Stamp Act in the House of Burgesses even as a young teenager, Thomas Jefferson looked on. Although often in disagreement with Henry and not entirely certain that the calls of "treason" that could be heard throughout the chamber were not correct, Jefferson was moved by Henry's oratory. Moreover he was aware, as was the rest of America, that it would be Virginia, the oldest and by far the largest colony, which would lead the protest.

In the years that followed, the colony did not feel the brunt of tax legislation as sharply as did the merchants of the Northern settlements. Still, Virginia organized a non-importation agreement in response to the Townsend Acts. This boycott, passed by a rump session of the House of Burgesses, was copied in all of the other colonies. But in those years, weather, more than Parliament, plagued Virginians. Torrential rains in May 1771 led to record flooding, destroying human and animal life as well as obliterating nearly 2.5 million pounds of tobacco, an estimated loss of £2,000,000.

The event which precipitated the crisis that would lead to Revolution occurred in Massachusetts on the night of December 16, 1773, when approximately 150 men, dressed as Mohawk Indians, boarded ships belonging to the British East India Tea Company and threw its cargo, 342 chests of tea, into Boston Harbor. British retaliation came rapidly. Parliament passed the Coercive Acts, called the Intolerable Acts in the colonies—a series of new laws that included closing the Massachusetts General assembly, shutting the Boston port upon which so many depended for their livelihood, and quartering British troops in the city.

Outraged by this perceived tyranny, the Virginia House of Burgesses attempted to pass a vote of sympathy. Disbanded by the royal governor before they could take that step, many of the burgesses moved down Gloucester Street to Raleigh's Tavern, where they met in a rump session. During this meeting, the burgesses voted to call for a Continental Congress, a gathering of representatives from all of the colonies to take collective action.

In September 1774, fifty-five representatives from twelve colonies met in Carpenter's Hall in Philadelphia. Virginia sent seven of its most prominent citizens—Peyton Randolph (who was appointed to lead the delegation), Richard Bland, Benjamin Harrison, Patrick Henry, Richard Henry Lee, Edmund Pendleton, and George Washington. Although not present, Thomas Jefferson prepared a document to guide the Congress's deliberations, entitled *A Summary View of the Rights of British America*. In it, he made clear the concerns of Virginians. While not advocating separation from the mother country, he called for an end to British-imposed taxes and a lifting of the band on western land settlement. Colonial resistance, through boycotts, had proved ruinous to Virginia's tobacco economy.

The first Continental Congress issued a statement of grievances and demanded Parliamentary repeal of all legislation passed since the end of the French and Indian War. Governor John Murray Dunmore repeatedly postponed calling the Virginia General Assembly into session in 1775. Finally, Peyton Randolph took the lead in organizing the Virginia Convention to meet in Richmond, well outside of Dunmore's seat of power in Williamsburg. Already certain that war was inevitable, Patrick Henry used this occasion to deliver his memorable speech, "Is life so dear, or peace so sweet as to be purchased at the price of chains and slavery? Forbid it, Almighty God! I know not what course others may take, but as for me, give me liberty, or give me death!" These were ironic words indeed coming from a slave-owner.

In May 1775, the Second Continental Congress convened once again in Philadelphia. Summoned back to Virginia to preside over a special session of the House of Burgesses that Dunmore had finally called, Peyton Randolph was replaced by Thomas Jefferson. The fighting at Lexington and Concord gave new urgency to the Second Congress, which authorized the creation of a Continental Army, appointing a reluctant George Washington to lead it. Most famously, Congress endorsed the Declaration of Independence written by Thomas Jefferson, one of the accomplishments of which he remained most proud. On Jefferson's tombstone on the grounds of his home at Monticello are carved the three things for which he wanted to be remembered—his authorship of the Declaration of Independence and the Statute for Religious Freedom (separating church and state), and his founding of the University of Virginia.

Mount Vernon in wintertime. Once home to George and Martha Washington.
CREDIT: The Mount Vernon Ladies' Association

But it was Washington, not Jefferson, to whom all colonists looked in 1776. Virginia's most famous son spent the next five years at the head of a ragtag army, engaging British forces, for the most part, outside Virginia. There was sporadic fighting in the colony during the early years of the Revolutionary War, mostly involving British attempts to blockade ports and skirmishes with those loyal to the royal governor. Like the other colonies, now states, Virginia wrote a constitution and elected a new governor—Patrick Henry.

Hundreds of Virginians who remained loyal to Britain (and who also may have feared the seizure of their estates) returned to England in the early years of the wars. Initial lenient treatment of the Tories, as those loyalists were called, soon gave way to harsher punishment as the war went badly in the North as well as in Virginia. British forces captured Portsmouth and Suffolk even as raiding along the Chesapeake continued, with the Royal Navy seizing supplies and slaves. Thousands of other slaves took this opportunity to run away.

Despite the increasingly desperate situation in the Chesapeake region, Virginian eyes still looked to the west. As always, it was a question of land. George Rogers Clark persuaded Governor Henry to give him command of a small band of men, largely made up of frontier folk, accustomed to the backwoods and ways of Indian fighting. In the spring of 1778, Clark and his 178 men reached the site of present-day Louisville, capturing a number of former French, now British, outposts.

As Virginian populations grew in the west, the assembly voted in 1779 to move the capital from Williamsburg to the more centrally located Richmond. In that year also, Thomas Jefferson replaced Patrick Henry as governor. Although a genius in many ways, Jefferson proved a poor administrator. In his defense, the problems he faced were indeed formidable. Almost all of Virginia's militia had been committed either to fight with Washington's army in the North or to resist British invasion in the South. Large numbers of Virginians were among the prisoners of war taken when Charleston fell in 1780. But Virginians also contributed to the defeat of Colonel Patrick Ferguson at the Battle of King's Mountain as General Charles Cornwallis made his way toward capturing Charlotte in North Carolina.

Patriot sentiment forced Cornwallis out of Charlotte soon enough, but not before he gave it the name "Hornet's Nest." Another Virginian, "Light Horse" Harry Lee would lead the patriot forces against Cornwallis at the Battle of Guilford Courthouse in North Carolina. Virginia, however, was left defenseless, a fact made clear when Benedict Arnold led a raid from Portsmouth all the way to Richmond, destroying a number of buildings in the state capital before looting or putting to the torch everything in his path back to Portsmouth.

As Cornwallis's army marched through the Carolinas toward Virginia, General Washington dispatched the famous French commander, Lafayette, along with what limited numbers of men he could spare. Lafayette's arrival in Richmond prompted British forces on the south side of the James River to join Cornwallis in Petersburg instead. In any event, Governor Jefferson had ordered the capital moved to what he thought would be the comparative safety of the mountain community of Charlottesville.

Cornwallis sent the infamous Colonel Banastre Tarleton on a mission to take Charlottesville with instructions to capture the author of the Declaration of Independence, who was there along with Patrick Henry and other well-known patriot leaders. But Virginia spies got word of the plan, enabling Captain John Jouette, Jr., of the Virginia militia to undertake an arduous forty-mile ride by horseback to warn the legislature in time. Almost all escaped to Staunton, eluding British plans to arrest and almost certainly hang the lot of them.

The patriot situation seemed increasingly desperate when the French king, Louis XVI deployed a large French fleet under the command of the Comte de Grase. Cornwallis retreated to Yorktown hoping to meet British ships carrying much-needed supplies, after the long year he had spent fighting in the Carolinas and Virginia. Instead, he encountered the French fleet occupying the ocean in front of him and Washington's army, moving into Virginia at last, taking up position to his rear. Trapped on the peninsula, Cornwallis had no choice but to surrender on October 17, 1781.

Yorktown is often viewed as the end of the Revolutionary War. However, peace would not be achieved until 1783 and Yorktown was only one among many battles. The American patriots did not win the Revolutionary War. After all, the main

British force was still in New York. But England had grown tired of the conflict. The costly commitment of men added to the pressure of what was an extremely unpopular war at home—few Englishmen understood or supported the concept of their army being sent to kill fellow Englishmen—convinced the British to withdraw. No one in London believed the newly created United States could survive: Let the Americans have their democratic experiment. When it failed, the British would be back.

Chapter Seven
Forging a New Nation

The American Revolution succeeded in breaking the ties binding the colonies to Great Britain largely through the efforts of the frontier farmers and middle-class merchants who made up the ranks of Washington's army. The Virginians hungry for land in the west were not the descendents of English Cavaliers, many of whom remained entrenched in the Tidewater. Rather, they were Scotch-Irish and Presbyterian, joined by increasing numbers of Baptists, having little enough in common with the Anglican oligarchy who were determined to retain their political and social prominence. But the planter class became more and more a minority while Jefferson encouraged the aspirations of the frontiersmen.

Thomas Jefferson's Statute for Religious Freedom, with its separation of church and state, faced a tough fight in the legislature, but eventually prevailed in 1786:

> Be it enacted by the General Assembly, That no man shall be compelled to frequent, to support any religious worship, place, or ministry whatsoever, nor shall be enforced, restrained, molested or burthened [sic] in his body or goods nor shall otherwise suffer on account of his religious opinions or belief; but that all men shall be free to profess, and by argument to maintain their opinions in matters of religion, and that the same shall in no wish diminish, enlarge or affect their civil capacities.

With this statute, Virginia set the example of the importance of secular government to American democracy.

St. Paul's Episcopal Church in Richmond.
CREDIT: Kathren Barnes

An equally crucial issue in Jefferson's mind was education for all, a cause for which he wrote his Bill for the More General Diffusion of Knowledge. Here he met with less success, and it would not be until after the Civil War that public education would become widely available in Virginia. Still, the concept of using state funds to support decent educational opportunities had been introduced into the public arena for debate and would come to fruition elsewhere before returning to Virginia.

Virginia's most significant contribution to the survival of the early republic came not from Jefferson but from his friend, James Madison. The Articles of Confederation drafted by the Second Continental Congress in 1777 to form a government to fight the war proved insufficient to the cause of surviving the peace, particularly in face of a British boycott aimed at ensuring economic hardship designed to crush the young republic. Shay's Rebellion in Massachusetts was the watershed event, convincing many of the nation's leaders, most importantly George Washington, perhaps the only genuine national hero whom all respected, that the time had come to form a new government.

Ostensibly to reform the Articles of Confederation, representatives from the states met once again in Philadelphia in 1787. Twelve states sent delegates. Rhode Island, sensing what was in the wind and fearing the loss of the one state–one vote rule of the Articles of Confederation, which had given this small state more political power than its population numbers warranted, stayed away. The remaining representatives met in secrecy, with Washington elected to preside.

The quiet, studious Madison had already drawn up a new plan of government. But he was considered too young (he was thirty-six) and frankly too lackluster to introduce the matter. Therefore it fell to a distinguished Virginian of impeccable family credentials, Edmund Randolph, to open the Constitutional Convention by introducing a resolution to abolish the Articles of Confederation. Instead, "a national government ought to be established, consisting of a supreme Legislative, executive, and Judiciary."

The Virginia Plan, as it would later come to be called, proposed a two-house legislature. The lower house would be elected at large and its numbers based on proportional representation; that is, the higher a state's population, the more representatives it could send. The lower house would elect the upper house. By far the largest state in the Union, Virginia would have dominated the lower house and, in time, the upper house as well under this plan. The smaller states—Delaware and New Jersey—foresaw a Virginia coup in this scheme. The

North feared a Congress dominated entirely by the South. Various compromises were discussed, with final resolution lying in a plan by which the upper house of the Congress would be elected by state legislatures (the Senate as it existed until the ratification of the Seventeenth Amendment in 1913).

The large populations of the Southern state were based on their extensive numbers of slaves. To gain Northern approval, the Constitutional Convention decided on the 3/5 Compromise; that is, black people would be counted at three-fifths of their populations. The rationale used was that slaves could not be expected to work with the industry of a free man and therefore contributed less to the overall economy. A specious argument but one accepted by Virginia and the other Southern states to achieve Northern acquiescence to the Constitution.

Far less attention was paid to the other two branches of government. Article III of the Constitution established a judiciary with a Supreme Court. As for the presidency, there was only one man who had the support of the entire nation. George Washington was elected by acclamation.

Acutely conscious of the sectional divisions between North and South, which had been present since the founding of colonies in the Chesapeake and Massachusetts Bay, Washington formed his new government carefully. The first cabinet was made up of four members. For his Secretary of Treasury, Washington selected Alexander Hamilton, a trusted aide from his days as a general. Though born in the West Indies, Hamilton had married into one of the wealthiest families in New York. General Henry Knox of Massachusetts, another trusted comrade-in-arms was Washington's nomination to be Secretary of War. With two northerners now in the cabinet, Washington chose two southerners to fill the remaining posts. Not surprisingly, he turned to Virginia for those men, making Thomas Jefferson Secretary of State and Edmund Randolph Attorney General.

Of all the problems facing the new national government, the most pressing was one of debt, some $54 million in addition to state debts totaling $20 million. To find money and gain the allegiance of wealthy Americans to the new government, Alexander Hamilton introduced his "Report on the Public Credit" to Congress. This plan included the creation of a national bank that would pay all debts, including those of the states, in full. To gain the monies necessary to do that, Hamilton proposed selling bonds.

In the years that had followed the American Revolution, speculators had been buying up soldiers' pay vouchers, a sort of chit or IOU issued by Congress, which had never been redeemed. Often paying as little as fifteen to twenty cents on the dollar, these speculators stood to gain a considerable profit with the settlement of the debt which included the government making good on those vouchers. To achieve that wealth, they were willing to invest in federal bonds. This gained the nation much-needed revenue and equally important, in Hamilton's eyes, the loyalty of the wealthier classes who must, of necessity, support the new government lest they lose their investment.

Others disagreed, notably James Madison and the Jeffersonians, or antifederalists as they came to be called, who found this betrayal of the common man to be at odds with the fundamental principals for which they had fought a revolution. But the money was needed and Congress eventually passed Hamilton's plan. Virginians found what victory they could in securing another compromise—a promise that a new national capital would be built on the banks of the Potomac between the states of Maryland and Virginia. The necessary ground was secured and construction of Washington, D.C., begun.

The outbreak of the French Revolution in 1789 only deepened the growing divisions between the followers of Hamilton, the federalists who favored a strong central government, and those of Jefferson. The bloody atrocities going on in France reinforced federalist lack of faith in the masses. By contrast, the antifederalists supported the concept of states' rights. Virginia had led the country for so long; it was only natural that these men looked to their state first. They also adopted Jefferson's well-known faith in the yeoman farmer as the backbone of the nation.

Although all continued to fear political parties, or "sects" as they scornfully referred to them, as dangerous to the survival of the republic, the separation between these two groups, largely along sectional lines—North versus South—was becoming obvious. Stepping down after two terms as president, Washington set one of the many precedents of his presidency by making a farewell address. He used that occasion to warn the country to avoid sectionalism and political parties.

Succeeded in office by his vice president, John Adams, Washington returned to Mount Vernon on the banks of the Potomac to live out his final years. Adams, a committed federalist, was doomed to a one-term presidency, largely by the machinations of his fellow federalists. Desperate to keep control of the national government, the federalists forced through Congress a series of legislation, including the Alien and Sedition acts. These laws were used to squelch newspapers loyal to Jefferson and his followers and deport others likely to vote for them.

Throughout United States history, few Americans have read the Constitution with care. They do, however, possess a gut understanding of its basic principles. The outrageous power grab attempted by the federalists boomeranged badly, producing two principal results. The first was Virginia's leadership in securing passage of the Virginia and Kentucky resolutions threatening secession as a final course of action if these laws were not withdrawn—the threat of secession was a notable option of opposition, setting a dire precedent for the future. Second was the overwhelming vote for Thomas Jefferson to become president of the United States in 1800.

Monticello: Thomas Jefferson's Little Mountain as it appeared after restorations in the mid-twentieth century.
CREDIT: The Virginia Chamber of Commerce Collection (The Library of Virginia)

The election of 1800 marked the start of twenty-four years of Virginians in the presidency, a period sometimes referred to as the Virginia Dynasty. Jefferson's experience as governor had left him with a profound distaste for administrative office and indeed, he spent as little time in Washington as he could, retreating to his home at Monticello near Charlottesville for long periods. Nonetheless, his administration produced three principal events of lasting national significance.

The first was a court case, *Marbury v Madison*, occasioned when newly appointed Secretary of State James Madison refused to deliver all of the "midnight appointments" to the bench made by John Adams in the final hours of his presidency. William Marbury applied to the Supreme Court for a writ of mandamus directing Madison to deliver the promised appointment as a justice of the peace in the District of Columbia. The Court's role as arbiter and its decision established the important legal principal of judicial review implied under the Constitution.

Second was Jefferson's purchase of the Louisiana Territory. One of the more fortuitous accidents in American history, Jefferson had dispatched three envoys to France to purchase the port of New Orleans. Having little enough interest in the Western Hemisphere and burned by the 1801–2 revolts in Haiti, Napoleon was willing to sell New Orleans but only if the Americans agreed to buy all of Louisiana, a vast expanse of land, the boundaries of which were disputed by Spain, determined to hold onto their North American possessions. Spain insisted Louisiana included only those lands along the Mississippi River (present-day states of Arkansas, Louisiana, and Missouri). Jefferson countered that the territory stretched south to the Rio Grande and westward to the Rocky Mountains, outlining a debate that would be settled only with the Mexican War four decades later.

Congress had authorized the American envoys to spend as much as $10 million to buy New Orleans, but Napoleon demanded $15 million for all of Louisiana. Dispatching one of their party back to America to seek permission, James Monroe and Robert Livingston remained behind, eventually agreeing to Napoleon's price.

Politics being as notoriously contentious in the nineteenth century as they are today, Congress debated the purchase ferociously, delaying its ratification. Ironically, the president who insisted upon a strict construction of the Constitution and a limited federal government used the power of that central government to double the landholdings of the nation (an inconsistency he justified by insisting he had made a treaty with France, a prerogative the Constitution did grant him). But it is clear that Jefferson was acting in the best interests of the country, not just as a Virginian. The Commonwealth had ceded the land claims originally made under charter and by conquest to all territory north and west of the Ohio River. The designation of Kentucky as a separate state in 1781 further reduced Virginia's claims in the West. Thereafter until 1863 (when West Virginia broke away to establish itself as a separate state), Virginia boundaries extended only to the Ohio River.

Jefferson's accomplishment stands as one of the most important events in American history. It acquired some of the richest and most beautiful land in today's United States. Equally important, the Louisiana Purchase made clear that America was destined to be a two-ocean country, stretching from the Atlantic to the Pacific. From only thirteen colonies hugging the Atlantic Seaboard in 1776, the United States had grown at an incredible rate in less than three decades.

Having bought it, Jefferson wanted to know more about this new land. To that end, he organized an expedition to be led by two Virginians, William Clark, younger brother of Revolutionary War hero, George Rogers Clark, and Meriwether Lewis, the president's personal aide. Like Jefferson, these men were not only Virginians but also hailed from Albemarle County. Clark had been born at Buena Vista, about two miles east of Charlottesville; Lewis came from Ivy, approximately seven miles to the west. The adventures of Lewis and Clark are probably among the best known in American folklore.

The impact of their exploration all the way to the Pacific Ocean was profound in establishing future American claims to the Oregon Territory still held by Great Britain. Equally important, on their return journey, the party found South Pass in what is present-day Wyoming. Like the Cumberland Gap in Appalachia, South Pass provided a route through the Rocky

Mountains that wagons could navigate, a vital discovery to future American expansion along the Overland Trail. Lewis and Clark also devised a term for the plains they had crossed. Deeming the area dry and useless for farming, Lewis and Clark called it the Great American Desert, a term that survived for the rest of the century. It was a barrier, in their view, to the richer lands that lay beyond.

This so-called desert land of the Louisiana Purchase sealed the fate of Indian peoples in the East. Now the United States government had a place to send those remaining Indian peoples whose presence barred American expansion into coveted farmlands east of the Mississippi. In what are now Oklahoma and Kansas, Indian peoples could be confined to reserves located on land no white man would ever want. Having grown up among the Cherokee, Jefferson was sympathetic to the pressures on them and undertook a policy designed to assimilate them as quickly as possible in order to protect them. This period from approximately 1801–25 is sometimes known as the Cherokee Renaissance, those years when the Tsalagi adopted Anglo-American dress, housing, land ownership, government, and economy—some even became slave owners. None of that would save them, of course, from Andrew Jackson

For other Indian peoples, Jefferson followed the policy of gradualism first developed by George Washington and Henry Knox, using treaties, cash payments, and intimidation to force "voluntary" removals westward. Jefferson's successors, Madison and Monroe acted similarly. The defeat of Tecumseh and the Shawnee at the Battle of Tippecanoe at the hands of American forces led by another Virginian, William Henry Harrison opened the Northwest Territory for Anglo-American settlement. It also precipitated the War of 1812.

James Madison, born at Port Conway in King George County, Virginia, built his home at Montpelier in Orange County, not far from Jefferson's Monticello. Serving for two terms as Jefferson's secretary of state, he succeeded him as president in 1809. The Congress also elected in 1808 contained a number of men who believed (falsely) that the British were continuing to push Indian tribes to attack frontier settlements. British insistence on stopping American ships at sea to search and usually confiscate both men and cargo added more fuel to increasing cries for war with Britain. Believing that the British had their hands full in fighting Napoleon, the War Hawks, led by Henry Clay of Kentucky and John C. Calhoun of South Carolina, argued that the United States should take this opportunity to secure remaining British territory in North America, including Canada.

On June 18, 1812, Congress passed a declaration of war. Madison felt the country was ill prepared, but chose not to oppose the majority vote. As in the American Revolution, a number of Virginians played significant roles in the conflict, including Commodore Lewis Warrington and Captain Robert Henley in the navy as well as William Henry Harrison, Winfield Scott, and Edmund Pendleton Gaines of the army.

But Virginia faced the same problem in this war as she had in the American Revolution. Her coastline was long and all too vulnerable to British attack. Although Virginians were able to repulse British naval attempts to seize Norfolk, they could not defend so much territory. British raiding parties once again destroyed a large number of valuable estates, seizing slaves and setting fire to the fields.

After Napoleon's final defeat at Waterloo in 1814, the British were able to turn the full brunt of their considerable military might against the Americans. Moreover, the British who were sent to quash the Americans were seasoned military men who had adopted the new tactics and strategies of war developed by Napoleon and his adviser, Henri de Jomini. This included capture of the opponent's capital as a primary target designed to destroy civilian morale. To that end, the British planned a three-pronged attack that included sailing into the Chesapeake. On August 24, 1814, they marched into Washington, burning the capitol and the president's home. Already peace delegates from both sides had commenced their negotiations in Belgium. The resulting Treaty of Ghent declared peace, establishing the United States boundaries at precisely where they had been at the war's outset and paid to put American ambitions to acquire Canada.

Like his predecessors Jefferson and Madison, James Monroe, the last in the series of presidents in the Virginia Dynasty period, eschewed European concerns. A native of Westmoreland County in Virginia, Monroe was sixty-one years old when he took office and seemed, in his dress and deportment, to be a relic of an earlier era. But Monroe looked to the future. Concerned about renewed sectionalism, which had erupted during the Hartford Convention in 1814, when the issue of secession had once again reared its head among the New England states, Monroe tried to draw the country together, appointing John Quincy Adams as his secretary of state. Madison had served as Jefferson's secretary of state; Monroe had held that office under Madison—it was viewed as the stepping-stone into the presidency.

Soon after his inauguration in 1817, Monroe undertook a goodwill tour of the country, beginning in New England and traveling as far west as Detroit. He was greeted at every stop by enthusiastic crowds and was indeed so successful in restoring national unity that he was reelected in 1820 with only one electoral vote cast against him (done by an elector determined that Washington would remain the only president ever elected unanimously). In his self-appointed role as a champion of American nationalism, the president issued his famous Monroe Doctrine in 1823, declaring that the Western Hemisphere was "henceforth not to be considered as subjects for future colonization by any European power." To defend

America's sphere of influence, the United States would go to war if necessary. Quid pro quo, the document also promised that "our policy in regard to Europe . . . is not to interfere in the internal concerns of any of its powers."

Monroe's principal concern may have been fears that Britain would try to seize Cuba from Spain. But British territorial ambitions were turning elsewhere in the nineteenth century. Indeed, the British navy upheld the doctrine's declaration that over three hundred years of European colonization in the Western Hemisphere were at an end. And the Monroe Doctrine, while little used in the decades following its pronouncement, would be frequently cited as precedent for twentieth-century United States foreign policy, particularly in the Caribbean.

Chapter Eight
Education and the Public Virtue

The hard-won democratic society in America believed that the success of their republic lay in fostering ideals of republican virtue in their children. As early as 1765, John Adams had written that liberty could only be protected by "knowledge diffused generally through the whole body of the people."[1] Jefferson's ideal of publicly funded education was supported by a similar plan proposed by Benjamin Rush to provide comprehensive primary and secondary schooling for all children, encouraging young men to attend college where the curriculum emphasis lay in the liberal arts—literature, history, and philosophy. However the vast majority of Americans, farmers for the most part, would support only primary education, rejecting the essential elitism of further schooling. Their teenagers were needed to work the fields or find a trade as an apprentice.

In Virginia, a number of colleges were founded in the years of the early republic including Hampden-Sydney and Washington Academy, later renamed Washington College, both organized in 1776. Today Hampden-Sydney remains one of two institutions of higher education in the country that accepts only men, while Washington College is now the coeducational Washington and Lee University.

William and Mary predated the Revolutionary War and remained the preeminent college in Virginia to be joined by the University of Virginia, which Thomas Jefferson began in 1819 in a design he called an "academical village." Jefferson's blueprints included ten pavilions whose upper stories were to be used as faculty homes, with downstairs classrooms. Two rows of individual rooms for students attached by a colonnade would underscore the village of learning that was at the core of Jefferson's vision. The university opened in March 1825 with 123 students including author Edgar Allan Poe. During that first year, Jefferson hosted student dinners at Monticello on the mountain overlooking the campus. He counted his founding of the university among the three most significant accomplishments of his life.

A number of academies at Norfolk, Petersburg, Winchester, Fredericksburg, and other sites provided education for Virginia's young men. America's first Methodist academy, Ebenezer School, was established in Brunswick County in 1790. The location of these institutions in northern and eastern Virginia makes clear that they were established for the benefit of planters' sons who could afford the tuition. No provision was made for the vast majority of Virginians, black or white.

Jefferson's dream to provide public primary education for all fell on deaf ears in the early years of the republic, coming to fruition after 1820 and then only in the North as reformers worked hard to force state legislatures to fulfill the guarantees of most state constitutions to use public resources to fund at least primary schools. Farmers and laborer taxpayers agreed that their children should be taught the three R's—reading, 'riting, and 'rithmetic.

In many homes, the job of educating the next generation fell to the mothers, and it was to these women that the responsibility of instilling republican virtues in their children fell. To provide education for women, considered necessary for them to rear the next generation, Virginia founded two academies in the antebellum period. In 1842, Augusta Female Seminary (later to become Mary Baldwin College) was organized in Staunton. Three years earlier in 1839, the Virginia legislature granted permission to seven citizens of the small town of

An aerial view of "Academical Village."

CREDIT: Richard Rummel, 1907 (Virginia Historical Society)

Farmville to create another seminary for the education of women. Following the lead of Northern communities which, in the absence of any public funding, raised their own monies, a joint-stock company, the Farmville Female Seminary Association sold shares at $100 each to secure the $30,000 necessary to build the academy, which opened its doors on July 17, 1843. During that first year, the school term consisted of only five months with a curriculum that included English, Latin, Greek, French, and Piano. Class fees were $15 for senior English, $12.50 for lower-level English, $5 for each foreign language, and $20 for piano. Room and board charges came to $10 per month.

Mathematics and science were soon added to the curriculum, along with history, geography, and philosophy. Like so many of the women's academies, Farmville Female Seminary grew slowly, becoming a college in May 1860, granting Mistress of Arts degrees. The course requirements for degree were:

- Six terms of English language and literature
- Six terms of French
- Two terms of ancient geography
- Six terms of Latin
- Two terms of geometry
- Three terms of Roman history
- One term of philosophy
- One term of chemistry
- Three terms of algebra
- Courses in religion and logic[2]

The outbreak of Civil War in 1861 impeded the development of academic institutions throughout the country as young men signed up to fight, some wearing the Blue and others donning the Gray. Their sisters remained at home, in many cases to provide labor necessary to keep the family farms

The doomed Ruffner Building at Longwood University. It was founded in 1839 as Farmville Female Seminary, but destroyed by fire in 2001, rebuilt in 2005.
CREDIT: Kathryn Blackwell

going. Some women assumed new roles as nurses, a calling for which Florence Nightingale had proven women's suitability and effectiveness during the Crimean War a few years before.

In the aftermath of war, women found opportunities open to them in professions previously reserved to men. This included secretarial work (the typewriter was invented during the war years) and, most especially, teaching. Farmville College was renamed the State Normal School for Women in 1914. A decade later, it was more appropriately renamed the State Teachers College. In 1949, the school became Longwood College although it continued to be regarded as—and in many ways still is—the state teachers college. Opening its doors to

The front parlor of the State Normal School for Women.
CREDIT: Kathryn Blackwell

men in 1976, Longwood University exists today as one of the leading centers of higher education in Virginia. Given its long history in teacher preparation, it is commonly said that there is not a student who passes through the public education system in Virginia who has not been taught by a Longwood graduate.

As suggested by the curriculum listed above, education in Virginia before the Civil War remained confined to liberal arts instruction, a luxury only wealthy families could afford. No provision was made for black or Indian children; nor were opportunities afforded for the vast majority of the population of small farmers. The latter saw no value in studying Latin, in any event.

The Morrill Land Grant Act of 1862 made public lands available and the proceeds were to be spent developing agricultural and mechanical colleges. Virginia's first land grant institution was Virginia Polytechnic Institute, commonly known as Virginia Tech. Founded in 1872, its purpose was the "education of the industrial classes," defined as "those who handled the tools or worked in the fields, mines, or workshops."[3]

Today, Virginia Tech exists as the largest institution of higher education in Virginia with some 25,600 students. Its motto, *Ut Prosim*, "That I May Serve" still reflects the republican ideals of Jefferson and other founding fathers.

In 1908, yet another school for women was organized in Fredericksburg—the State Normal and Industrial School for Women. Later renamed Mary Washington College in honor of George Washington's mother, who spent most of her life in Fredericksburg, the campus is home to approximately thirty-five hundred students.

During the Reconstruction era, the new black governments throughout the South were anxious to provide long overdue educational opportunities for African-American young people. With financial help from the Freedman's Bureau, philanthropists, and some religious groups, the Hampton Normal and Agricultural Institute began construction of its campus in 1868. Ten years later, Hampton Institute opened its doors to Indian students as well. Along with Carlisle in Pennsylvania, Hampton was one of the schools to which so many Indian children were sent as part of the United States acculturation policy to separate Indian children from their parents and confine them in institutions where they could be assimilated into white culture. Children from over forty Indian nations were sent to boarding school at Hampton between 1878 and 1923.

Today, Hampton University is a thriving educational institution with over five thousand students.

America's first fully state-supported institute of higher education for blacks was founded in Petersburg on March 6, 1882. In 1920, the land-grant program for black students moved from Hampton, where it had been located since 1872 to this new campus called Virginia Normal Collegiate Institute. In 1979, the school was renamed Virginia State University.

Virginia has many other fine colleges and universities, including George Mason in Fairfax (named for George Mason, author of the Virginia Bill of Rights, which was used as a model for the United States Constitution's first ten amendments); James Madison University (named for the nation's fourth president) in Harrisonburg; Christopher Newport University in Newport News (named for the captain of the *Sarah Constant* who led the first English settlers to Jamestown); as well as an extensive network of community colleges. The capital, Richmond, is home to two of Virginia's finest universities: Virginia Commonwealth University and the University of Richmond. VCU is divided into two campuses—the Academic Campus located two miles west of Richmond's historic Fan District, and the Medical College of Virginia. First organized in 1838 as the medical department of Hampden-Sydney College, MCV received state affiliation in 1860. The University of Richmond began as a Baptist Seminary in 1830, transforming itself into a comprehensive liberal arts college in 1840.

During the Civil War, Richmond College served as a hospital for Confederate soldiers and later as barracks for Union troops. Indeed, the Civil War disrupted education throughout the South, but especially in Virginia, where so much of the fighting took place. Even before the outbreak of war, however, all of the academies in the state experienced sharp declines in enrollment, a reflection of the overall failing economy. Virginia had tied its fortune to tobacco and the slave system

The Stephen Putney House. Today Putney houses the offices of the president of the Virginia Commonwealth University.
CREDIT: Kathren Barnes

necessary to work those fields. The Commonwealth would pay a heavy price for its dependence on a single cash crop and its practice of slavery.

Notes

1. Gordon S. Wood, *The Creation of the American Republic, 1776–1787* (New York: W. W. Norton & Co, 1969), 570. See also David W. Robson, *Educating Republicans: The College in the Era of the American Revolution, 1750–1800* (New York: Greenwood Press, 1985).
2. Robert Badenhop, Kathryn Blackwell, Kathleen Costello, Jason Knause, Sherry L. Livingston, Robyn Olson-Goodman, Sandra Pleva, Megan E. Wade, and James Wahlgren, *Longwood: A Campus and a Community*, edited by Marshall Hall, James Jordan, and Deborah Welch (a project of the Longwood University Public History Program, available on compact disk, 2001), 76.
3. Duncan Lyle Kinnear, *The First 100 Years: A History of Virginia Polytechnic Institute and State University* (Blacksburg: VPI Educational Foundation, 1972). See also Peter Wallenstein, *Virginia Tech, Land-Grant University* (Blacksburg: Pocahontas Press, 1997).

Chapter Nine
The Peculiar Institution

No one was more aware of the dichotomy between their public pronouncements on the blessings of liberty and the continued practice of slavery than were the Virginians who dominated the First and Second Continental Congresses as well as the Constitutional Convention of 1787. George Washington wrote "... there is not a man living who wishes more sincerely than I do to see a plan adopted for the abolition of [slavery].[1] In *Federalist Paper 54*, James Madison denounced slavery as a "barbarous policy." Thomas Jefferson agreed, writing in his *Notes on the* State *of Virginia* that the practice of perpetual servitude destroyed the morality of both master and slave. Such passionate pronouncements coming from men who continued to own slaves seems at best ironic. At worst, it appears as a hypocrisy that condemned generations of black men and women to suffer.

These Virginian leaders were sincere, however, in their distaste for slavery and all too aware of its discrepancy with the ideals of the Enlightenment upon which they based their republic. Many Virginians practiced manumission, freeing their slaves in their wills—a sort of fire insurance for the judgment they would face in the hereafter. George Washington, left such provisions in his will, liberating the few slaves he still held. Virginia led the way among the Southern states in creating laws making it easier for men to free their slaves.[2]

The evidence seems to suggest that many Virginians, as did most Americans, thought—or at any rate hoped—that slavery would die out as the republic continued to evolve, securing the rights of liberty for all men. James Madison, for one, believed there existed growing sentiment throughout the Commonwealth to abolish slavery. In fact, the Virginia General Assembly debated a number of antislavery petitions in the decades of the early republic. The most popular senior thesis topic at the College of William and Mary during the early nineteenth century was devising a way by which southerners could be compensated and blacks given their liberty.

And yet slavery continued. Even Patrick Henry, one of the few who dared to defend the practice openly, conceded that he deplored slavery, but "I see that prudence defends its absolution."[3] Thomas Jefferson framed the problem more clearly in his famous statement, "We have the wolf by the ears, and we can neither hold him, nor safely let him go."[4] In his *Notes on Virginia*, Jefferson had written at length about his belief that blacks were inferior to whites, a condition he blamed on their years of enslavement rather than any inherent distinction. Nonetheless, the reality remained and Jefferson feared that, if given their liberty, blacks would face the same fate that American Indian peoples had suffered—forced removal or even, as it seemed to him in the early nineteenth century, extinction.

Jefferson's concerns about race hatred were not so far-fetched. Indeed, subsequent history has shown enmity to be one of the continuing legacies of this country's long practice of slavery. But his words have more often been misinterpreted to substantiate arguments that Virginia was concerned about possible black retribution against their former white masters. Most observers of slavery during the antebellum period agree that slavery was practiced in Virginia in its mildest form. It seems a cruel oxymoron to call any form of slavery mild. Still in Virginia, numbers were declining even as the practice of slavery grew throughout the South. But the presence of so many blacks fascinated foreign travelers. David Montague Erskine, later the second Baron Erskine, visited Norfolk in 1798, writing in his diary, "One half or more of the inhabitants are black, and slaves . . . Out of ten thousand inhabitants, five thousand are slaves who work for the white people . . . it is not at all uncommon for a white to keep blacks to let out as horses are in England."[5] Eli Whitney's invention of the cotton gin in 1793 would vastly increase the profitability of slavery and thereby cement its practice throughout the cotton-growing states.

Virginia, by contrast, experienced an economic decline in the first half of the nineteenth century; its population slipping to 949,000 whites and free blacks by 1850. Of those, only 114 Virginians possessed plantations so large that they owned as many as one hundred slaves.[6] The vast majority of the Commonwealth was made up of small farmers, men who worked their own land, laboring hard on soil that had been worn out by so many years of tobacco cultivation. That spent land accounts as much as anything for the emigration of people away from Virginia during the antebellum period, seeking richer grounds to the west.

Yet, slavery was practiced and, in a state marked by its rural society, blacks often outnumbered whites. Living on these isolated farms, people feared the possibility of slave revolts. Sporadic uprisings during the colonial period had set a precedent and the stories of Haitian resistance to their French overlords (the same bloody resistance that convinced Napoleon to sell Louisiana) fed fear among white farmers. Yet, Virginians seem to have convinced themselves that the atrocities happening hundreds of miles away on a small island in the Caribbean could never be duplicated in their midst.

That complacency ended abruptly in 1800 with an event known as Gabriel's Insurrection. This incredibly ambitious plot was undertaken by two men, Gabriel, a slave on a Henrico County plantation owned by Thomas Prosser, and his fellow planner, a slave by the name of Jack Bowler. The lines of communication these two men were able to establish, involving perhaps a thousand slaves scattered on plantations from Petersburg to Charlottesville, seems truly incredible. Similarly breathtaking was the scope of their ambition to undertake a massive killing of whites and seize the capital at Richmond. Word of their plans leaked out, however, enabling Governor James Monroe to summon the militia into action, thwarting the plans of Gabriel's army. Jack Bowler was captured almost immediately, as was Gabriel several weeks later. Both were hanged along with thirty-five others who were found guilty of taking part.

At the same time, others brought to trial were found innocent and allowed to return to their plantations, evidence that the fears produced by this event did not reach the level of hysteria. The plan had come to nothing in the end. Still, Gabriel's Insurrection made a strong impact on Virginians, destroying the fledgling Abolition Society of Virginia and nearby Maryland. As a precaution against future plots, a permanent guard was posted in Richmond. Those groups who had established small schools for black children were discouraged from continuing their work. It was literacy, after all, that had enabled Gabriel and Bowler to coordinate their plans.

Despite the harsh punishment meted out to the leaders of Gabriel's Insurrection, slave revolts, albeit on a much smaller scale, continued, one occurring in Norfolk only two years later. Many white Virginians feared the continued presence of free blacks in the Commonwealth although there was no evidence of their participation in either event. In 1806, the General Assembly passed a law ordering any newly manumitted black to leave the state within the year; a harsh ordinance later amended to enable local courts to give permission for freed blacks to stay provided they could prove their good character. In fact, Virginia had little choice. The states surrounding Virginia passed laws forbidding any freed slave from the Commonwealth to cross their borders.

This question of what to do with the black population had been central to the thinking of Jefferson, Madison, and others. Various schemes for deportation were debated, always without resolution. In the end, Virginia, along with the other Southern states, continued to practice slavery.

One particularly harsh solution involved the sale of Virginia slaves further south. As the tobacco economy continued to decline after 1800, Virginia had less need for slave workers. By contrast, the thriving cotton fields in more Southern states required labor—and Virginia supplied it. Slavery may have been mild in Virginia, but the state's culpability in sending men and women to the far harsher conditions of those cotton fields in the Deep South must be acknowledged. Still, at a constitutional convention and later in meetings of the state legislature between 1829 and 1832, Virginia gave serious consideration to compensated emancipation, largely at the urging of non-slave-holding Virginians in the western part of the state. None of these measures passed, in large part because no way could be found to pay the owners during those decades when the state was suffering its own financial woes.

The Commonwealth's declining economy and loss of population reduced Virginia's influence in national affairs during the Jacksonian Era of the 1820s and 1830s. State pride did not acclimate easily to this new diminished role, and the collective bruised ego was especially sensitive to Northern demands, trying to dictate how Virginians should handle what they viewed as very much their own business.

The growing divisions between the North and South were further exacerbated by the diatribes printed in Northern abolitionist press; some of which encouraged slave revolts and the spilling of Southern blood. The most vitriolic of these writers, William Lloyd Garrison, editor of the *Liberator*, warned repeatedly of the revenge southerners would suffer at the hands of their slaves if they refused to emancipate them. In January

1831, Garrison printed a long poem, including the following stanza:

> Woe if it come with storm, and blood, and fire,
> When midnight darkness veils the earth and sky!
> Woe to the innocent babe—the guilty sire—
> Mother and daughter—friends of kindred tie!
> Stranger and citizen alike shall die!
> Red-handed slaughter his revenge shall feed,
> And Havoc yell his ominous death-cry;
> And wild Despair in vain for mercy plead—
> While Hell itself shall shrink, and sicken at the deed![7]

Garrison stops short of actually encouraging blacks to revolt, but his words were ill-received among Southerners. The danger was brought home to Virginians in perhaps the most famous slave revolt in American history—Nat Turner's Rebellion.

A self-proclaimed mystic, Nat Turner began his rampage in Southampton County on the night of August 22, 1831. With a band of fellow slaves numbering perhaps as high as two hundred, Turner led his followers to slaughter his master and the entire family before moving on to neighboring plantations, killing men, women, and children. Many of the bodies were mutilated, some decapitated. Once again, the state militia was called into action. Bands of white civilians took action also, seizing, sometimes torturing any black with whom they came into contact. One company of men killed forty blacks in one day, cutting off the heads of fifteen of them and setting them on pikes, partly in revenge for the atrocities Turner's band had committed, but more as a warning to any other slave considering revolt.

Turner was captured and hanged, along with nineteen of his followers. But this event was far different from Gabriel's Insurrection three decades earlier. Fifty to sixty people had died

HORRID MASSACRE IN VIRGINIA.

The Scenes which the above Plate is designed to represent, are---Figure 1. a Mother intreating for the lives of her children. ---2. Mr. Travis, cruelly murdered by his own Slaves.---3. Mr. Barrow, who bravely defended himself until his wife escaped. ---4. A company of mounted Dragoons in pursuit of the Blacks.

Just Published, an Authentic and Interesting

NARRATIVE

OF THE

TRAGICAL SCENE

Which was witnessed in Southampton county (Virginia) on Monday the 22d of August last, when FIFTY FIVE of its inhabitants (mostly women and children) were inhumanly massacred by the Blacks!

Short and imperfect sketches of the horrid massacre above mentioned have appeared in the public Journals, but the public are now presented with every particular relative thereto, communicated by those who were eye witnesses of the bloody scene, and confirmed by the confessions of several of the blacks while under sentence of death.

A more shocking instance of human butchery has seldom occurred in any country, and never before in this—the merciless wretches carried destruction to every white person they found in the houses, whether the hoary head, the lovely virgin, or the sleeping infant in the cradle! they spared none!—a widow (Mrs. Whitehead) and her 10 children were murdered in one house! among the slain on that fatal night, was an amiable young lady but 17 years of age, who the day following was to have been united in marriage to a young gentleman of North-Carolina, who had left home the evening preceding with the expectation of conveying there the succeeding day the object of his affections! but, alas! how sad was his disappointment! he was the third person who entered the house after the horrid massacre, to witness the mangled remains of her whom he was so shortly to espouse! The Blacks after having completed their work of death, attempted to evade the pursuit of those who had collected to oppose them, by secreting themselves in a neighboring swamp, to the borders of which they were pursued by a company of mounted dragoons. Of the fifty five slain nearly two thirds of the number were children, not exceeding twelve years of age! and it was truly a melancholly scene (as was observed to the writer by one who witnessed it) to behold on the day of their interment so great a number of coffins collected, surrounded by the weeping relatives!

While the friends of humanity however or wherever situated, cannot but sincerely and deeply lament the awful destruction of so many innocent lives, yet, the humane and philanthopic citizens of New-England, and of the middle States, cannot feel too thankful for the repose and peace of conscience which they enjoy, by wisely and humanely abolishing laws dooming a free born fellow being (without fault or crime) to perpetual bondage!—an example truly worthy of imitation by our brethren at the South.

The Narrative (which contains every important particular relating to the horrid massacre) is afforded for the trifling sum of 12 1-2 Cents. ☞ This paper left for perusal, and to be returned when called for.

This broadside, describing Nat Turner's Rebellion, circulated throughout the Northern States between 1831 and 1832.

CREDIT: Virginia Historical Society

at the hands of Turner's band in 1831. The Virginia legislature, called into immediate session, debated furiously, condemning slavery in no uncertain terms. Virginia wanted to be rid of it. Indeed, Governor John Floyd wrote in his diary at this time, "Before I leave this Government I will have contrived to have a law passed gradually abolishing slavery in this state."[8]

But he was not successful. The old impediment to emancipation remained: where were the freed blacks to go? As the panic over Turner's Rebellion began to subside, Virginians looked for a scapegoat, finding one readily enough in William Lloyd Garrison and the abolitionist societies of the North. Laws were passed throughout the South making it illegal to sell the *Liberator*. Governor Floyd went so far as to demand Garrison's extradition to stand trial and, when the governor of Massachusetts refused, he actually offered a bounty for Garrison's capture and delivery to Virginia "dead or alive."

Fearing further slave insurrections, debate in Virginia's General Assembly went on at a fever pitch. Early bills introduced by a number of delegates, including Thomas Jefferson's grandson, Thomas Jefferson Randolph, and Thomas Marshall, son of Chief Justice John Marshall, to abolish slavery were squelched. Instead, "black laws" were established, equally applied to all blacks, free or slave. These limited freedom of movement and assembly, even for religious services, except under carefully monitored conditions. Penalties were particularly harsh for any black found carrying a firearm. These legislative debates of 1831–32 constituted one of the most tragic missed opportunities in American history. Those who sought to handle the situation by making slavery harsher shouted down the proponents of gradual emancipation.

It was left to a professor at William and Mary to provide the arguments defending slavery, establishing a pseudo-intellectual posture to which Southerners would cling in the remaining decades before the Civil War. Thomas R. Dew's *An*

Essay on Slavery offered scriptural justifications as well as Constitutional guarantees to private property. He went further, denouncing emancipation plans as impracticable and even proclaiming slavery a vital economic component of American civilization.

Nat Turner's Rebellion put an end to the debate over colonization. Free blacks in Virginia had been prominent in the effort to resettle American blacks in the newly created Liberia in Africa. Lott Carey, a tobacco factory worker, had purchased his own freedom and that of his family. He then studied for the ministry, joining the first settlement of blacks who set out for Liberia in 1821. Some white Virginians had participated actively in this effort as well—it seemed the only answer to a culture that was not prepared to live side by side with large black populations.

But these proponents of colonization disappeared after 1832, and the resulting sale of many of Virginia's slaves to the Deep South seemed, at least in the worried minds of many, to reduce the danger. Still, new laws were passed for the protection of whites. Tough restrictions on manumission were added to legislation making it a crime to teach a slave to read or write. Emancipation disappeared as a thesis topic for students at William and Mary.

Virginia had chosen its course, chaining itself to slavery, allying itself with its fellow Southern states. Jefferson once called slavery the "rock on which the union would split." The coming decades would prove him right.

Notes

1. Letter to Robert Morris, April 12, 1786, found in W. B. Allen, ed., *George Washington: A Collection* (Indianapolis: Liberty Classics, 1989), 319. The classic study of Virginia slavery remains Edmund

Morgan, *American Slavery, American Freedom: The Ordeal of Colonial Virginia* (New York: W. W. Norton and Company, 1995).

2. James H. Kettner, *The Development of American Citizenship, 1608–1870* (Chapel Hill: University of North Carolina Press, 1984), 302.

3. Jonathan Eliot, *The Debates of the Several State Conventions* (Philadelphia: Lippincott, 1937), 3: 590.

4. Jefferson writing to John Holmes, April 22, 1820, found in Thomas Jefferson, *Writings* (New York: Library of America, 1984), 1494.

5. Robert McColley, *Slavery and Jeffersonian Virginia* (Champaign: University of Illinois Press, 1964), 57–58.

6. Virginius Dabney, *Virginia: The New Dominion* (New York: Doubleday and Company, 1971), 254, 275.

7. Ralph Korngold, "Woe If It Comes with Storm and Blood and Fire," *Portraits of America,* Stephen B. Oates, ed. (Boston: Houghton Mifflin Company, 1991), 1: 260.

8. Dabney, 275.

Chapter Ten
North and South: A Nation Divides

Although very much a Southern state, Virginia diverged sharply in its economy from the rest of the South in the decades preceding the Civil War. Slave populations declined in the state while, in the rest of the South, they continued to increase. In some counties in South Carolina, blacks outnumbered whites ten to one by 1860. As Virginia had done during its first century of English settlement, most of the rest of the South, particularly the Deep South, formulated its economy around a single cash crop. King Cotton ruled in Georgia, making the port of Savannah one of the largest import/export centers on the East Coast. New Orleans and Mobile served similar purposes for Alabama, Louisiana, and Mississippi.

The exhaustion of the land in Virginia, depleted by centuries of tobacco planting, demanded change. New crops were introduced to replenish the soil. The system of crop rotation that the early Jamestown settlers had observed Indian people using was adopted and proved successful. In the Tidewater area of the southeast, grain became a major source of income. Other families turned to raising livestock, especially cattle and hogs. The Shenandoah Valley and the Piedmont area proved good land for orchards, especially for the growing of apples. Resourceful farmers used those apples to produce cider. Alcohol brought in significantly greater profits than mere fruit.

The 1840s also witnessed the beginning of a migration of farmers from Pennsylvania and other states above the Mason-Dixon Line into northern Virginia. They brought with them new techniques of farming, relying upon free rather than slave labor. Their success reinvigorated land prices in Fairfax and other counties in the northern part of the state.

Virginia also turned to manufacturing in the 1850s, establishing some 4,841 industrial enterprises by 1860. Indeed, by the time Virginia seceded from the Union, she possessed the fifth largest industrial economy in the nation, another factor setting her apart from the rest of the South and its reliance upon agriculture.

Still, the state that had once led the nation in size, population, and the wealth of its minds now lagged behind. The long years when the Virginia Dynasty had captured the presidency and set the standard of statesmanship by which all other politicians would be measured had passed. Only in the South was Virginia still able to consider itself a leader, and the old "Cavalier" pride helped to ally Virginia with the Southern cause as sectional debate heightened in the 1850s.

In the North the plantation owners' cause was labeled with a more enflamed epitaph—Black Power. America suffered an unceasing series of political crises in the 1850s that tumbled the country into a final split, bringing about the civil war that men like Washington and Jefferson had feared would eventually happen.[1] The nation first came close to war over the issue of admitting California to the Union. Crisis was avoided by Congressional passage of a series of laws known as the Compromise of 1850, including a new and rigorous fugitive slave act.

Two years later, Harriet Beecher Stowe, "the little woman who made this great war," as Lincoln would later call her, published *Uncle Tom's Cabin*. The efficacy of this work lay not in its morbid, very Victorian storyline and prose, but in the ease with which it lent itself to the stage. Although the book was outlawed in much of the South, Northern audiences flocked to productions where they could witness the cruelty of Simon

Legree, the peril of Eliza leaping across the ice floes trying to reach safety beyond the Ohio River, and the sufferings of the saintly slave, Uncle Tom. The cruelty of slavery was brought home to northerners, many of whom had never met a black person. Slavery was regrettable, of course, but it existed far away to the South, or so most Northerners had always reassured themselves. Stowe pricked the conscience of a nation, swelling the abolitionist movement.

Many Americans, including Virginians in the Whig Party, continued to hope that some means might yet be devised to rid the nation of this blight. They believed that, if contained, slavery would eventually die out. But the new lands opening in the West challenged those traditional boundaries of slavery.

Stephen Douglas's introduction of the Kansas-Nebraska bill in 1854, based on the notion of popular sovereignty, opened the door to the West. The fight between pro-slavers and free-soilers led to the violence of Bleeding Kansas in the years that followed. While condemning "Black Power" (a reference to the power of plantation owners) of the South as responsible for that debacle, Senator Charles Sumner of Massachusetts was attacked by a young congressman from South Carolina. The "caning of Charles Sumner" by Preston Brooks on the floors of the United States Senate only confirmed the barbarity of Southerners in Northern minds. The Dred Scott decision issued by a Supreme Court dominated by Southern members in 1857 reiterated the status of slaves as property. It also threw both the Missouri Compromise and the Northwest Ordinance out the window. Southerners were now free to take their slaves into the North.

That few would have any reason to do so was beside the point. Southern power had won the day in 1857, convincing many northerners, including a young politician from Illinois, Abraham Lincoln, that the South had been allowed to have its own way too often, exuding a prominence in national affairs unwarranted either by its population or the morality of its slave system. The Whig Party died in the debate over the Kansas Territory. In its place, there arose a new political party, this one clearly sectional in its platform. The Republican Party took as its motto, *Free Soil, Free Labor, Free Men.*

One of the final crises of the 1850s, the one that convinced many Southerners they were no longer safe in the Union, took place on Virginia soil. Under cover of darkness on October 16, 1859, John Brown, along with a small party of men, including some of his sons, raided the small town of Harper's Ferry, seizing control of the federal arsenal there. They killed the mayor and took several hostages, including Lewis W. Washington, great-grandnephew of George Washington. Putting out a call for the slaves of Virginia to join them and take up arms, they barricaded themselves, along with their hostages, in the armory's engine house.

Virginia's governor immediately ordered the militia into action. He also appealed to the federal government, which responded, ordering Colonel Robert E. Lee to take a company of marines and secure the arsenal. The militia got there first. The fighting was fierce. Visitors to Harper's Ferry today may still view the bullet holes in many of the town's buildings, including its church. By the time Lee arrived, only Brown and four of his followers were still alive. Battering down the door of the engine house, Lee's men captured Brown.

A series of misjudgments followed. Brown was brought to trial in Virginia, charged with treason, murder, and inciting slaves to revolt. Finding him guilty on all charges, the presiding judge, Richard Parker, sentenced him to death. Governor Henry A. Wise had the power to intervene. On his desk lay at least nineteen affidavits sent by people who knew Brown, testifying to the fact that he was insane, or at any rate, unbalanced. Instead, Wise ordered the court's sentence to be carried out. Brown was taken to Charles Town, some miles away, and hung from the largest tree in the county on December 2. The tree still exists. Local farmers use the spot today to sell cider, cashing in on tourists who visit Harper's Ferry.

Had Governor Wise lived up to his name, he would have used the evidence in his possession to have Brown committed to an institution for the insane. By executing him, he turned John Brown into a martyr, one who had died for the cause of abolitionism and, moreover, had been killed by the state of Virginia.

Northern treatment of Brown as a saint enraged the South. After all, here was a man whose purpose had been to incite slaves to rebellion, repeating the horrific killings of Nat Turner. Virginians, in particular, were offended that their state was singled out for blame. Virginian parents who had sent their sons to Northern universities now demanded that they return home. Efforts were made to meet Northern propaganda efforts with equal prose. Virginia pointed out that no slaves had responded to Brown's call to join him. Moreover, the first man killed by Brown's forces had been a free black, a railroad employee. So much for Brown's altruistic principles—the man wanted to spill Southern blood.

Those arguments fell on deaf ears in the North. Governor Wise responded by calling upon Virginians to become self-sufficient, boycotting Northern goods in favor of home-grown products. Indeed, Wise made clear his secessionist sentiments in a series of speeches he gave during his final months in office.

On January 1, 1860, a new governor, John Letcher, took his place. Long a critic of slavery, Letcher faced a hostile assembly in the aftermath of the Brown Raid. Eschewing his earlier principles, he joined those who espoused the cause of slave ownership. Still he hoped to calm the secessionist sentiment Wise had aroused, proposing a national convention in which all the states could come together and find some resolution for their differences.

Events were soon to overtake those who, like Letcher, hoped to avoid war. Later that year, Abraham Lincoln was elected president of the United States. Only 1,921 Virginia votes had been cast for the Republican Party's nominee and most of those came from western counties now in West Virginia.[2] Still, the Democratic candidate, Stephen Douglas, didn't carry Virginia either. Instead, the Commonwealth, by a slim majority, voted for John Bell of the Constitutional Union Party, hoping to avoid war.

In response to news of Lincoln's election, the South Carolina legislature met on December 20 and unanimously passed an Ordinance of Secession. Six other states quickly followed suit. By February 1, 1861, all of the cotton states had seceded from the union—Alabama, Florida, Georgia, Louisiana, Mississippi, South Carolina, and Texas. Virginia continued to try to avert war. The legislature finally acted on Governor Letcher's call for a convention to be presided over by ex-president John Tyler, also a Virginian. Meeting in Washington, the convention proved to be a dismal failure, with few states sending any delegates. But Letcher soldiered on, calling a state convention on February 13. To be sure, there were secessionist proponents among the representatives in attendance. Nonetheless, on April 4, the convention passed a resolution to stay in the Union.

A week later, South Carolina took the final step, opening fire on Fort Sumter. It was a Virginian, Edmund Ruffin, who received the honor of lighting the canon fuse for that first shot on April 12, beginning the bombardment. Even then the Virginia legislature still refused to act. But the major Richmond newspapers were howling for war. On April 14, Sumter fell and President Lincoln issued a call for volunteers to put down the rebellion. Virginia could hesitate no longer. By a vote of eighty-eight to fifty-five, the state convention voted to follow the rest of the South out of the Union. The Stars and Stripes was lowered; the flag of the Confederacy now flew over the state house.

On April 18, Robert E. Lee was offered command of the federal army. After a long night of consideration, he declined the appointment, sending instead his resignation. It would fall to a fellow Virginian, General Winfield Scott, who first rose to prominence during Cherokee Removal and later from his command during the Mexican War, to accept briefly the post as head of the United States Army. Lee, first accepting command of Virginia's ill-prepared militia, would be called upon a year later to lead the Army of Northern Virginia. The fellow Virginians now prepared to do battle against one another in what many (but not Lee) believed would be a short conflict. The next four years of the bloodiest war in American history proved how wrong they were.

Notes

1. The best treatment of the events of this decade remains Michael Holt's *The Political Crises of the 1850s* (New York: W. W. Norton and Co, 1983). For other classic studies of this era, see Eric Foner, *Free Soil, Free Labor, Free Men* (New York: Oxford University Press, 1995), David Morris Potter, *Impending Crisis* (New York: Perennial, 1977), and James M. McPherson, *Battle Cry of Freedom: The Civil War Era* (New York: Oxford University Press, 2003).
2. Virginius Dabney, *Virginia: The New Dominion* (New York: Doubleday and Company, 1971), 290.

Chapter Eleven
The Blue and the Gray

A Mississippian, Jefferson Davis, was elected president of the newly organized Confederate States of America with a Georgian, the poet Alexander Stephens, chosen to serve as his vice president. Nonetheless, Virginia would be at the forefront of the war. The Confederate capital was moved to Richmond. Much of the fighting in the four years that followed would take place on Virginia soil. Indeed, one of the ironies of this war is that the two states perhaps most reluctant to leave the Union—Virginia and North Carolina—would be called upon more than any others to sacrifice their sons to this conflict.

In command of the ragtag recruits who responded in large numbers to join the army in Virginia, Robert E. Lee realized the state faced the same problems that had threatened the Commonwealth during the American Revolution and the War of 1812—that long coastline so vulnerable to invasion. The South had no navy worthy of the name. Before leaving Norfolk, the Union scuttled what warships remained in the harbor to prevent them from falling into Confederate hands. Burning a few buildings, they left the rest of the dock intact, enabling Virginians to salvage badly needed cannon and powder stored there.

Equally vulnerable was Virginia's long northern border. The disaffection of the western part of the state was manifest. The long struggle between the Tidewater planters and the small farmers of the west would come to a head during the war when West Virginia broke away, forming their own state.

Lee ordered what armaments remained at Harper's Ferry moved to Richmond. He also summoned cadets from Virginia

Military Institute to begin training the volunteers into a functioning fighting force. He was aided by a talented cadre of officers who included Thomas J. "Stonewall" Jackson and J. E. B. Stuart. Many of the commanders of the Confederate Army throughout the war hailed from Virginia, among them was A. P. Hill, Jubal Early, Richard Ewell, Lewis A. Armistead, Richard S. Garnett, James L. Kemper, and even George Pickett, a native of Richmond. Lee would need these men in the long struggle ahead against an enemy that would always have superior numbers and supplies.

Lee's basic strategy was to fight a defensive war, leaving the North to mount their invasions, repelling them whenever and wherever he could. The first attack came in July as General Irvin McDowell crossed the Potomac. General Johnston moved approximately ten thousand men from the Shenandoah to reinforce Beauregard at the small town of Manassas, taking up positions at a creek known as Bull Run. A series of blunders on both sides marked this first battle, the Confederate forces nearly outflanked by McDowell's troops. That is when General Jackson made his stand on Henry House Hill, refusing to be moved. South Carolinians on the scene that day were ordered by their commander to join the general: "There stands Jackson like a stone wall. Rally behind the Virginians!"[1]

Jackson's determination turned the tide of battle, sending the Union troops scurrying back through the lines of civilian carriages, including congressmen and their wives, picnic baskets at the ready, who had come out from Washington to watch.

The rout of federal troops produced a panic among the onlookers who made their way back across the Potomac as best they could. Jackson wanted to take a force and follow, invading the capital. Lee ordered him to stand down, fearing those forces McDowell still had in reserve.

This early success marked the beginning of two years of Southern resistance to Northern offensive maneuvers. The

The White House of the Confederacy. Formerly a private residence, the house was purchased in 1982 by the Confederate Government and was occupied during the war by President Davis and his family. Today called the Museum of the Confederacy, it houses a memorial room for each of the 13 Confederate states and features a wide variety of objects and material from the era. In front of the mansion is the propeller shaft of the first Confederate ironclad, the U.S.S. Merrimac, *whose engagement with the* U.S.S. Monitor *revolutionized naval warfare in "The Battle of the Ironclads" of 1862.*

CREDIT: Kathren Barnes

An 1861 photograph of Cub Run, VA. The bridge was destroyed by the First Battle of Manassas, also known as Bull Run, the first major battle of the Civil War. The Confederates named the battle after the nearest town, Manassas, while the Union named the battle for the nearest physiographical feature.

CREDIT: George N. Barnard

Civil War cemetery markers at Manassas Battlefield as they appear over 150 years later.

CREDIT: Landace Lowe

Part of the battlefield as it appears today.
CREDIT: Landace Lowe

A house at Manassas.
CREDIT: Landace Lowe

A historical guide plaque honoring the dead at the First Battle of Manassas.
CREDIT: Landace Lowe

South was unable to win all skirmishes in which forces were engaged, but they denied the Union a climatic victory that would have ended the war. Moreover, the South developed a new weapon—the ironclad ship. Raising the *Merrimack* from where the Union navy had scuttled her in Norfolk harbor, workmen covered her sides in armor plate, renaming her, the *Virginia*. In 1862, the *Virginia* sailed out of Norfolk, sinking the Union ship, the *Cumberland*, and capturing another warship, the *Congress*.

This development marked the end of the days of wooden shipping, but it was not enough to secure a Confederate victory. The federal ship, the *Monitor*, similarly outfitted with metal plating, also had a revolving gun turret atop it and could sail in more shallow water. A pitched battle between the two ships resulted in a draw with both taking up defensive positions. The *Virginia* protected the James River and any assault on the Confederate capital by sea, while the *Monitor* acted as a watchdog for the rest of the Union navy blockading the coast.

That blockade prevented badly needed supplies from reaching the Confederacy either from Britain or France, while English textile mills cried out for Southern cotton. By 1860, the South had supplied 90 percent of the cotton on the world's markets. Without it, those British mills were forced to cut back and some even closed, throwing thousands of men onto the streets. The timing could not have been worse. The potato blight that had first appeared in Ireland during the 1840s continued to plague its farmers, forcing mass immigration of young people in search of new jobs to save themselves and bring the remainder of their families out of Ireland as well. With its textile industry at a standstill, Britain had no employment to offer, compelling the Irish to seek refuge elsewhere—in New Zealand, Australia, and America.

The North had little use for the Irish who had been streaming across the Atlantic in "coffin ships" for over a decade. Viewing them as unclean and, most damning of all, Catholic, the overwhelmingly Protestant North closed its doors to these immigrants. But as the war stretched on into its second year, Northern enthusiasm to join the fighting dropped off sharply. Those large Irish boys found work filling the Union ranks. Many would die in this desperate attempt to find the cash to get their families out of Ireland.

Throughout 1862, Union forces continued their plans to capture Richmond. Taking York and Norfolk, the federal army forced a Confederate retreat up the James River. By May 24, McClellan's men were so close to the capital that they "were able to set their watches by the sound of Richmond's clocks."[2] Among Southern forces, General Joseph E. Johnston's severe wounds at the Battle of Seven Pines compelled Jefferson Davis to name Robert E. Lee to replace him as commander of the Southern forces. While Lee was beginning to fortify the capital, Stonewall Jackson was achieving much needed morale-boosting victories in the West, forcing Union troops out of the Shenandoah Valley. Alarmed by these events, Lincoln withdrew the reinforcements McClellan had requested to take Richmond, committing them to the Valley Campaign instead.

Despite Jackson's victories and the colorful escapades by which "Jeb" Stuart's moved through the Union ranks to join Lee in Richmond, the Army of Northern Virginia remained severely outnumbered with supplies running low as well. The factories of the North outfitted the Union armies with armaments; Lee had to rely on the Tredegar Iron Works at Richmond alone for his ordinance. The numbers of dead and wounded grew. Nearly sixteen thousand men were brought to the hospitals in Richmond during June 1862. The largest hospital, Chimborazo, lay approximately one mile east of the Capitol and therefore only a short distance from Hollywood Cemetery, where so many of these soldiers, Union and Confederate, would be laid to rest. Howard's Grove on the Mechanicsville

Turnpike was the second largest. Despite growing shortages of surgical instruments and drugs, the doctors and nurses were able to achieve remarkable survival rates. Still, thousands died. A lack of medical knowledge and the overwhelming numbers combined to make it impossible to treat all of them. However, Richmond had been saved for the time being.

Chasing the new federal commander, General John Pope, northward, Stonewall Jackson did much to raise Southern morale by seizing the enormous supply depot Pope had created at Manassas. Filling first their empty bellies and then freight cars with barrels of flour, pork, and other foods as well as clothing, Jackson's army sent the train southward. Meanwhile Lee ordered General James Longstreet to the northern border. He attacked Pope's army at Chantilly in Fairfax County, securing an overwhelming victory and forcing Pope, who had vowed to crush the Confederates, back across the Potomac.

Hoping to take advantage of this wave of victories, Lee went on the offensive, taking the Army of Northern Virginia into Maryland with plans to cut Union rail lines there. If he could secure Maryland for the Confederate cause, Lee's plan was then to attack Washington or Philadelphia, to achieve some resounding victory that would convince the North to break off the war. On September 17, he engaged Union forces at the Battle of Antietam, one of the bloodiest in the war. But the federal army held strong and Lee was forced to withdraw.

McClellan did not follow, losing an opportunity to defeat Lee's army. Nonetheless, Lincoln seized the victory at Antietam to issue his Emancipation Proclamation, freeing those slaves in areas still under Confederate control. While, this made very little immediate difference to most slaves, it offered an important propaganda tool. The war was now cast clearly as a conflict of right versus wrong—a war to end slavery. It is doubtful, in any case, that the Confederacy would have found an ally among the European nations. Britain may have been starved for Southern cotton, but the Prince Consort, Albert, an avowed liberal and implacable foe to slavery, stood in the way. Following his death from typhoid, his grieving widow, Queen Victoria would brook no discussion of any policy that ran counter to her beloved husband's views.

The South was on its own, most of its infantry marching barefooted by the end of 1862. Morale remained remarkably high, but Southern pride could not match Northern industry nor overcome Lincoln's determination that the Union would not be divided. Still, Lincoln needed a general who would fight. He replaced McClellan with General Ambrose Burnside who took the Army of the Potomac into Virginia once again, moving toward the small town of Fredericksburg in November 1862. In December, Burnside bombarded the town with a barrage of artillery, reducing much of it to rubble, while his infantry was crossing the Rappahannock on pontoon bridges. What remained was sacked by the federal troops.

Lee and Jackson combined their forces, taking up position on the heights outside Fredericksburg. A dense fog hid both armies from each other. When it lifted at last, Burnside must have seen the impossibility of the situation he was facing. The Army of Northern Virginia stood entrenched behind a stone wall. Nonetheless, Burnside ordered the attack, sending wave after wave of infantrymen across the sunken road in front of the Confederate positions. Overwhelming carnage followed as rebel cannon and rifles mowed those Union troops down. Over twelve thousand Union soldiers were killed or wounded along that front.

Burnside retreated under cover of darkness, and Lee, like McClellan at Antietam, did not follow. He, at least, had better reason. Still vastly outnumbered, Lee had to protect the men he had left. The North could find fresh troops; Lee could not. He was low on supplies as well.

Even civilians were beginning to go hungry by the third year of the war. Food, clothing—everything was in short supply. Southerners compensated as best they could, drying sweet potato skins, pounding them into powder, and then brewing from that a drink that passed for coffee. Women went to work in the fields, growing black-eyed peas and other staple crops to feed their families.

The famous blockade-runners who made it through the Union naval lines did so with an eye to their own profits, shipping luxury goods instead of medicines, clothing, or food. Sixty percent of all Confederates wounded were being treated in Richmond where the doctors were forced to operate without instruments or drugs. Native roots were used as substitutes; even dinner forks and knives were pressed into service.

The plight of their families starving at home began to produce a high rate of desertion among Confederate forces. Some deserters were caught and shot, but few men could be spared to hunt them down. Most who reached their homes stayed there. Others, after getting a crop in the field, returned to continue the fight.

But the situation was growing increasingly hopeless. Lee had never believed the Union would let the South go. He watched helplessly as his men fell ill with diseases, dysentery being the most virulent, produced by their inadequate diet. Lacking feed, the South began to lose horses as well. Virginians watched as their beloved mounts died off, leaving few to move the artillery or serve the cavalry.

Following the debacle at Fredericksburg, which had resulted in the recall of Burnside. General "Fighting Joe" Hooker was given command of the Army of the Potomac. He moved on Chancellorsville, to the west of Fredericksburg, in the spring. Stonewall Jackson attacked the federal forces there in May 1863. He achieved a spectacular victory, but it was to be his last. Shot by one of the Confederate pickets as he returned with a scouting party, Jackson's arm was amputated. At first there was some hope for his recovery, and at least time for his wife to travel to be with him. But pneumonia set in, killing him. The general's body was carried to Richmond, where it lay in state in the Capitol. Thousands passed by to pay their respects to one of Virginia's best-loved heroes before he was taken home to Lexington for burial.

In the spring of 1863, Union and Confederate cavalry units clashed at Brandy Station, near present-day Culpepper, in what would be the largest cavalry engagement of the war. In desperation, Lee determined to go on the offensive once again. He may have hoped to win another victory over Union forces, a follow-up to Chancellorsville that would convince the federals to ask for a truce.[3] More certain is that he was in search of much needed supplies. Jeb Stuart, whose job was to use his cavalry unit to scout out the position of the Union army and keep Lee informed, instead used his force to make a series of raids throughout the area. As a result, Lee had no idea of the whereabouts of the enemy.

On July 1, 1863, the two armies came face to face at Gettysburg. Union cavalry delayed the Confederate advance until infantry could arrive later that morning. Nonetheless, the federal army fell back through the town. Lee ordered General Ewell to advance on Cemetery Hill and to take the ground "if practicable." Jackson would have done it. Ewell hesitated, with devastating results. Union forces entrenched themselves on the ridge, as Lee and Jackson had done at Fredericksburg. The next day, July 2, Ewell finally made his attack even as Lee ordered General Longstreet to try and outflank the enemy forces on Little Roundtop. Both attacks failed. General George Meade, who had replaced Hooker in what by now seemed to be a revolving door of Union army commanders, arrived, fortifying the flanks in preparation for attack.

Lee saw no alternative but to order a charge directly against Cemetery Ridge where he hoped to break Meade's lines. Of the fifteen thousand Confederates who took part in Pickett's Charge on July 3, over nearly a mile of open field against well-entrenched Union forces, forty-five hundred of them were Virginians, including the First Virginia Regiment, which traced its origins back to the colonial period. The disastrous results are well known. Lee lost nearly one-third of his army in that defeat. The First Virginia Regiment suffered 80 percent casualties.

On the morning of July 4 (Independence Day—the irony was noted on both sides), the Confederate Army deserted the field. During their retreat back across the Potomac, they learned that Vicksburg, the last Confederate stronghold on the Mississippi had fallen, cutting the Confederacy in two. Taken together, these defeats marked the turning point of the war. In fact, it was doomed to failure from the moment Charleston opened fire on Fort Sumter. Yet the fighting would continue for nearly two more years at a staggering cost of human lives.

The victor of Vicksburg supplied Lincoln with the general he had long sought. Ulysses S. Grant was transferred east to take command of all Union forces. Technically, Meade remained in command of the Army of the Potomac, but Grant traveled with that army and gave the orders. Determined to move on Richmond and end the war as quickly as Lincoln wanted, Grant forced engagements with Lee's army in May during the Wilderness Campaign. This horrendous battle marked one of the more horrifying episodes of the war as a fire broke out, engulfing wounded soldiers lying on the battlefield. Many of them were still alive, helpless and screaming, as they burned to death.

Engaging Sheridan's cavalry at Yellow Tavern cost the life of Jeb Stuart, who remained a true hero among Virginians despite his failure at Gettysburg, because that failure was unknown to the general public. Hundreds gathered outside the

The Grant House in Richmond. It became a Sheltering Arms Hospital during the Civil War.

LEFT: *A Confederate wife and child left behind.* RIGHT: *A young Confederate cadet.*
CREDIT: Sherry L. Livingston, Recovered photographs from originals housed at Village View Plantation

home in Richmond where Stuart, wounded by a bullet in his abdomen, was taken to die. His wife, frantic to reach him in time, was cut off by federal troops. Her husband could hear the sounds of fighting north of the city as he died.

Meanwhile, Union generals Phillip Sheridan and Franz Sigel continued their devastating raids throughout the Shenandoah Valley, burning homes and destroying crops. Both Virginia Military Institute and Washington College were put to the torch. Sheridan, whose later atrocities against Indian peoples in the wars on the Plains secured him a well-earned brutal reputation is best remembered in Virginia today for the policies he ordered to be carried out in the Shenandoah. Sheridan himself has left a record of his destruction of the Valley:

Cary Street in Richmond after Union soldiers burned the Confederate capitol in 1865. Few photographs of the ruined city exist today.

A postcard, postmarked 1911, depicting a bustling Cary Street, approximately 50 years later.

The whole country from the Blue Ridge to the North Mountains has been made untenable for a rebel army. I have destroyed over 2000 barns filled with wheat, hay and farming implements; over seventy mills filled with flour and wheat; have driven in front of the army over 4000 head of stock, and have killed and issued to the troops not less than 3000 sheep. A large number of horses have been obtained. . . . Lt. John R. Meigs, my engineer officer, was murdered beyond Harrisonburg near Dayton. For this atrocious act, all the houses within an area of five miles were burned.[4]

Still trying to prevent Grant from reaching Richmond, Lee's army dug in at Cold Harbor. Federal troops engaged in trench warfare also, developing a new mode of fighting that would be repeated decades later in World War I.

Union armies converged on Virginia from all sides as Sheridan was ordered to break off his destruction of the Shenandoah and join in the attack on Petersburg and Richmond. Sherman was marching through the Carolinas and approaching from the South. Lee sent word to President Davis that both cities would fall soon. On April 2, 1865, Richmond was evacuated, the capital moved to Danville in the western part of the state. Setting the warehouses on fire to prevent supplies from falling into Union hands, the retreating Confederate Army watched as strong winds spread the fire quickly, engulfing the city. Entering federal troops were finally able to get the conflagration under control, enabling President Lincoln to travel down on April 4, holding his son Tad's hand as he stood amidst the ruins of what had been the Confederate capital.

Lee retreated westward, hoping to make contact with General Joseph Johnston in North Carolina. Grant caught up with him at Saylor's Creek, just east of the town of Farmville. In a running battle, Grant killed or captured nearly half of Lee's force and almost all of his remaining supplies. Pursuing him through Farmville and on to Appomattox, which lay twenty-five miles to the west, Grant surrounded what was left of Lee's army, later numbered at 28,231 officers and men who would be paroled after the peace treaty was signed.

In what appears today to be a damnable waste of life, the two armies fought on while Grant and Lee exchanged messages to work out the terms of surrender. Lee's intransigence at this point is particularly difficult to understand. The war was over and Grant was not ungenerous in his treatment of his defeated foes. Meeting at the home of Wilmer McLean in Appomattox, the two men stood about awkwardly, talking briefly about their joint service during the Mexican War, before signing the documents.[5] All Confederate enlisted men were allowed to return home immediately, each given a horse or a mule to speed their journey and provide them with a draft animal for spring plowing. Moreover, Grant made provisions available to feed those half-starved men. Grant did not even demand Lee's sword, the traditional symbol of surrender. Rather he let Lee keep what shreds of dignity he could still muster—and his pride. Virginia pride, Southern pride: it had taken them out of the Union and into a war that cost over six hundred thousand soldiers' lives. Many more would die after they returned home, of tuberculosis, dysentery, or starvation. Civilian casualties were high as well.

The stain of slavery had been removed from the American landscape. The abhorrent practice of perpetual servitude, the problem Virginia debated most often but had never devised an answer for, was over at last. But Virginia had paid a high price for its moral failure in allowing slavery to continue. Much of the state was destroyed, its population decimated. Those still alive emerged from the war as bitter survivors who blamed not their state leaders but the "Yankee" troops who were now on their soil and would remain there for the rest of the decade. Virginia, once the leader of the republic, was now a conquered province.

Notes

1. Virginius Dabney, *Virginia: The New Dominion* (New York: Doubleday and Company, 1971), 305.
2. Matthew Page Andrews, *Virginia: The Old Dominion* (Richmond: The Dietz Press, 1949), 497.
3. This motivation was endorsed by Michael Shaara in his best-selling book, *Killer Angels* (New York: Ballantine Books, 1987), the basis for the subsequent movie, *Gettysburg.*
4. Dabney, 347.
5. Ironically, McLean had moved his family from Manassas to Appomattox to get them away from the war. Those interested in learning more about the Civil War in Virginia should consult the work of James I. Robertson, Jr., Director of The Virginia Center for Civil War Studies and Professor of History at Virginia Tech. His books include *General A. P. Hill: The Story of a Confederate Warrior, Soldiers Blue and Gray, Civil War Sites in Virginia: A Tour Guide,* and *Standing Like a Stone Wall: The Life of General Thomas J. Jackson* among other work.

Chapter Twelve
Binding of Wounds

Of all the states in the Confederacy, Virginia emerged from the war most devastated. It had been the scene of so many battles: its lands had been ravaged, its crops destroyed, and its economic system thrown into disarray by the emancipation of the slaves. Even those parts of Virginia which had escaped the worst of the fighting found it difficult to continue. The 1865 grain crop failed and the harvest of 1866 was only partially successful. Most egregious of all was the loss of the next generation. Along with North Carolina, Virginia shares the dubious distinction of having given more of her sons to "The Cause" than any other Southern state.

In his second inaugural address in 1865, President Lincoln emphasized his determination to "bind up the nation's wounds." But his assassination in April left his vice president, Andrew Johnson, to try and carry out those policies of reconciliation. A hapless politician, Johnson proved to be no match for the Radical Republicans determined to punish the South and ensure the future of their own political party. The Reconstruction Act of 1867 divided the South into five military districts, each in the charge of a Union general. Virginia fell into Military District Number One under the command of General John M. Schofield.

Federal forces would remain in the state until 1870. While the army occupied much of the rest of the South until 1877, the troops left Virginia earlier because of the relative calm they perceived among the populace. To be sure, the Virginia General Assembly had passed Vagrancy Acts in 1865, alarmed by the growing numbers of former slaves wandering the streets of Richmond and other cities. Most of them, like many other Virginians, had been made homeless by the war and had nowhere else to go. But the long-feared retribution of blacks against their former owners never materialized. A few race riots broke out in Norfolk and Alexandria, but these were fought between blacks and Union troops. The Ku Klux Klan, formed to terrorize blacks, never achieved any real following in Virginia and largely disappeared from the state after 1868.

Like other Southern states, Virginia faced the disenfranchisement of most of its men, members of what became known as the Conservative Party (they feared the repercussions of calling themselves Democrats in the postwar years). As a result, a Republican government took charge. Two-thirds of the delegates to the Republican Convention in Richmond in April 1867 were black. Despite the handicaps produced by so many centuries of slavery, the black government worked surprisingly well. State roads were repaired and, perhaps most important to black parents, schools were constructed for the education of their children.

The Freedman's Bureau sent teachers South to staff these new schools. To the consternation of the white citizenry, these volunteers included *Uncle Tom's Cabin* as part of the required curriculum readings. They even organized their students to celebrate the fall of Richmond as a holiday. Still, on the whole, black government operated with far more success in Virginia than in other states. This participation extended to the local as well as the state level when former slaves were appointed to positions as justices of the peace and found work in such middle-class occupations as the police force.

The Virginians excluded from participation in their government divided into two camps. One, led by Robert E. Lee, urged reconciliation. Accepting a post as president of Washington College, renamed Washington and Lee College as the rebuilding of the destroyed campus began, Lee published calls for young men to stay in Virginia (many had already immigrated) and for all to embrace their former loyalty to the Union. But a great deal of bitterness remained, angry fires fed by General Jubal A. Early and the Reverend Robert L. Dabney, among others. The latter's vitriolic rhetoric gave vent to the feelings of many who refused to be reconciled to defeat: "What, forgive those people who have invaded our country, burned our cities, destroyed our homes, slain our young men, and spread desolation and ruin over our land? No, I do not forgive them . . ."[1]

As leaders of Virginia from before the war sought to regain both political and economic power within the Commonwealth, it was left to the women to bind the wounds. It was a task they had undertaken throughout the conflict. Much has been written about the struggles of Southern women to keep their homes intact while their men were away at war. Fearing the telegram that might (and probably would) one day come informing them they were now widows, and the ever-present danger of invading Union troops, these women soldiered on, trying to grow enough food to feed their children. Indeed, some women did take to the field as soldiers, disguising their identities, and donning the gray uniform, a story perhaps best known today in the Peter, Paul, and Mary song, "Cruel War."

> *The cruel war is raging*
> *Johnny has to fight.*
> *Oh how I long to be with him*
> *Both morning and night . . .*
>
> *I'll tie back my hair,*
> *Men's clothing I'll put on.*
> *I will pass as your comrade*
> *As we march along.*[2]

Colorful stories are told of Virginia women who acted as spies among Union troops, including Belle Boyd from the Shenandoah Valley, who socialized with Yankee soldiers, scandalizing her neighbors in nearby Martinsburg. But Belle was also gathering important information, which she passed along to generals Stuart and Jackson. Stonewall Jackson even sent her a note commemorating her contributions. Other women dedicated themselves to the care of the wounded. Most famous in Virginia was Sally Louisa Tompkins who, after the Battle of Bull Run, accepted the offer of a local judge to use his house in Richmond as a hospital. Naming the institution Robertson Hospital after her benefactor, Tompkins used her own monies to keep the twenty-two-bed facility open with a staff of only six. Still, she achieved a 94.5 percent survival rate, convincing Jefferson Davis to commission her as a captain in the Confederate Army so she could receive government funds to keep the hospital going.[3]

For the majority of women, however, the struggle to survive took precedence, a feat made all the more difficult by Sheridan's campaign of destruction in Virginia. In her diary, Nancy Emerson left an account of those raids:

> At one of our neighbors, they took every thing they had to eat, all the pillow cases and sheets but what were on the beds, & the towels & some of the ladies stockings. One of them made up a bundle of ladies clothing to take, but his comrade shamed him out of it. They then poured out their molasses, scattered their preserves & sugar & other things about the floor, & mixed them all together & destroyed things generally.

Elsewhere she writes of Union desecration of both churches and their cemeteries. But worst of all, "How have they soaked our soil with the blood of our noblest & best . . ."[4]

Yes, that was the worst of all—the loss of so many sons, brothers, and husbands. Virginia, following the Civil War, was a state of widows, women determined to preserve the memories of their husbands. More than that, they wanted to justify their loss and to that end, women assumed the responsibility of what historian, Bertram Wyatt-Brown has called "enshrining 'The Lost Cause.'"[5]

Throughout Virginia, women took on the task of honoring "Our Glorious Dead." It is difficult to find a city or town anywhere in the state that does not have at least one prominent monument to the Confederate soldier. The most striking example of the South's determination to honor "The Cause" can be found in Richmond, at Hollywood Cemetery. Located only a mile from the capitol building, the cemetery covers a vast expanse of ground along the banks of the James River to Cherry Street and beyond. First established in 1847 and designed in the garden landscape style that would become popular throughout America in the nineteenth century, the cemetery contains many tall trees and gently rolling paths that tourists today follow among the incredible barrage of monuments and crypts that are crowded together—a permanent example of Victorian era mourning with its large praying angels hovering over intricately carved tombstones.

Over sixty thousand bodies have found their resting places at Hollywood, among them the remains of eighteen thousand Confederate soldiers, two thousand reinterred from Gettysburg in 1872. Union soldiers are buried there as well, casualties who died in the nearby hospital. Virginia women tended those graves, perhaps in the hope that Northern women would do the same for Confederate men whose bodies lay somewhere far from home. The roses of Hollywood Cemetery are famous, an infinite variety of blossoms planted in honor of the dead on both sides.

TOP: *Sarcophagi of fallen Confederate soldiers at Hollywood Cemetery.*
BOTTOM: *The Archway to the Confederate Officers' Section of the Hollywood Cemetery, erected in 1918.*
CREDIT: Alyssa Holland

TOP: *Symbols of Victorian mourning customs, angels watch over the fallen soldiers in Hollywood Cemetery.*
CREDIT: Alyssa Holland

BOTTOM: *Veterans' Cemetery in Hampton, Va., an example of Confederate cemeteries often seen in Virginian towns.*
CREDIT: Rachel Blair

But it was the Confederate dead who, of course, received the lion's share of attention. The cemetery, perhaps more than any other site in the state, is a shrine to the fallen of the "Lost Cause." One of the most prominent structures is the Confederate Memorial, a ninety-foot granite stone (no mortar was used) pyramid constructed in 1869 at a cost of $25,000. The monument was erected in tribute, surrounded by many graves that are simply marked, "Unknown."

Twenty-three Confederate generals are buried at Hollywood, more than at any other site. The square stone arch marking the entrance to the "Confederate Officers Section, 1861–1865" was erected in 1918, proof of the staying power of the South's devotion to the memory of its Confederate dead. Here may be found the rather plain tombstone of First Lieutenant Isaac Newton. On the back of his marker was inscribed the poem:

Think of me when you are happy
Keep for me one little spot
In the Depth of Thine Reflection
Plant a Sweet Forget Me Not.

The enormous monuments in Hollywood Cemetery ensure that sentiment. Virginia's dashing cavalry leader, J. E. B. Stuart, and his family are buried at Hollywood, his graved marked by a tall obelisk. Far more elaborate is the shrine built over the grave of General George Pickett, famous for his disastrous charge at Gettysburg. Not far away lay the remains of Richard Garnett, who lost his life leading one of Pickett's divisions on July 3, 1863.

Two American presidents, both sons of Virginia, James Monroe and John Tyler, are buried at Hollywood, as is the president of the Confederacy, Jefferson Davis. More poignant is the grave of Davis's five-year-old son, who died falling from a balcony during the war. Lincoln's loss of his beloved son, Willie, while in the White House, is well known but few remember today that the Davis family suffered a similar tragedy. Testimony to the soldiers' loss of family can be found in the graves of three of James Longstreet's children, all victims of scarlet fever from January–February in 1863, only a few months before Longstreet carried out those fateful orders at Gettysburg.

One of the most famous memorials at Hollywood is the grave of a little girl who was just five years old when she died. A huge iron dog stands watching over the site. The story goes that the dog statue had been a fixture outside a Richmond store. The little girl always patted it whenever she accompanied her mother into the shop. At the time of her death in 1863, the South was desperate for iron. To save his dog from being melted down to make armaments, the storeowner donated it for the child's grave, where it remains.

Like all cemeteries, Hollywood possesses its fair share of ghost stories. The one that seems most appropriate to the setting concerns the statue of a widow mounted on top of her husband's tomb. On the anniversary of his death, the statue purportedly raises its head, looking at anyone watching, letting them see the tears streaming down its face. For the remainder of the year it remains prone in the widow's mourning position.

This monument symbolizes the South and perhaps especially Virginia. As the mourning continued, so did memory, which was kept alive deliberately and determinedly. Veterans of the war left requests to be buried in Hollywood. Lieutenant William M. Lawson, color-bearer of the First Virginia Regiment during Pickett's charge, lost his right arm that awful day in 1863 but lived on to 1910. His remains are interred at Hollywood, where he lies among the comrades with whom he had fought half a century earlier.

The Civil War has been described as a conflict of brother against brother. The poignancy of that observation can be found throughout Hollywood Cemetery. Typical is the case of Major General David Rumph Jones. A graduate of West Point in 1846, he went on to serve in the Mexican War, as did so many of the officers who would later take up arms against one another. He resigned his commission in 1861 to join the Confederate Army. He took part in the Peninsular Campaign, the Seven Days' Battle, and Sharpsburg before succumbing to heart disease in 1863. He is buried at Hollywood, his grave honored as one of the veterans of The Cause.[6]

As early as 1890, the first statewide societies of the Daughters of the Confederacy formed in Missouri and Tennessee, the latter as the Ladies' Auxiliary of the Confederate Soldiers Home. Ironically, the more famous Daughters of the American Revolution also points to 1890 as their year of origin. But the DOC provides clear evidence of long Southern memories: this organization exists to ensure that the sacrifice of Confederate soldiers is not forgotten. Their banner dedicates their society to "The Cause and Our Glorious Dead."

1890 also witnessed the commission of a statue of Robert E. Lee, which was originally to be placed in a field outside of Richmond. But the residents of the city objected and the sculpture was put downtown, beginning what became known as Monument Avenue. Six statues line the street today, four of them honoring Confederate heroes. Later, effigies of a navy captain and one of Virginia's most famous sons of a new century, Arthur Ashe, would be added.

In Virginia, it is not possible to forget the war, or as one very old lady of the Farmville community, now deceased, always called it, "the late unpleasantness." Beyond the memorials, battlefields, and cemeteries, numerous other commemorative sites abound, and many are open to the public, including the Stonewall Jackson House in Lexington, the only home Jackson and his wife, Mary Anna Morrison, owned. They lived there before the war while Jackson taught at nearby Virginia Military

Institute. Not far away, he lies buried in a cemetery. The Stonewall Jackson Shrine can be visited as part of the Fredericksburg and Spotsylvania National Military Park.

At many battlefield sites in Virginia, one may tour the cemeteries as well, the saddest of which may be at Appomattox. There lie the remains of the young men cut down in the final hours of war, even as Grant and Lee debated the terms of surrender. Nowhere is the sense of waste more evident than at Appomattox.

To come to terms with that loss, Southerners, especially Virginians, dedicated themselves to remembering "The Lost Cause" and "Our Glorious Dead." Almost every Southern family, including this author's, has some piece of memorabilia from that era. In this author's attic, there is a wooden cradle, crafted by a great-great-great uncle before he left his pregnant wife and answered the call to fight for the Confederacy. A dirt farmer, a man who had never owned a slave, nonetheless went to war and died, leaving a widow to raise the twin girls she bore, and to work the land as best she could.

Every Southern family has a story or two like that. The divisions between Southerners over the war continued well into the twentieth century. Some kept pieces like that cradle, and clung to the myth of states' rights and other rationales for why their men had to die and condemn them to a life of grinding poverty. Others did as Robert E. Lee advised: they put the past behind them, buckled down, and prepared to assume their place again in the Union and the New South, developing new economies based on free labor.

Notes

1. Virginius Dabney, *Virginia: The New Dominion* (New York: Doubleday and Company, 1971), 400.
2. *Peter, Paul, and Mary* (Warner Bros. Records, 1962).
3. Bell Wiley was among the first to write about the contributions of women to the war effort in *Confederate Women* (New York: Greenwood Publishing, 1975). See also Drew Gilbert Faust, *Mothers of Invention: Women of the Slaveholding South* (Vintage, 1997); James M. McPherson, *For Cause and Comrade: Why Men Fought in the Civil War* (New York: Oxford University Press, 1998); and Catherine Clinton, *Divided Houses: Gender and the Civil War* (New York: Oxford University Press, 1992).
4. Diary of Nancy Emerson, excerpts taken from entries of July 13, 1864 and March 6, 1863, found at a website entitled, "A Tribute to Confederate Women" (www. Geocities.com/sre_33/).
5. Bertram Wyatt-Brown, *The House of Percy: Honor, Melancholy, and Imagination in a Southern Family* (New York: Oxford University Press, 1996).
6. For more information, see Chris Ferguson, *Hollywood Cemetery, Her Forgotten Soldiers: Confederate Field Officers at Rest* (on line) or visit the website at www.historicrichmond.com/hollywood.html. See also Mary Mitchell, *Hollywood Cemetery: The History of a Southern Shrine* (Richmond: Virginia State Library, 1999). For a good study of Virginia's women and the role they played in keeping Confederate memories alive, see John M. Coski and Amy R. Feely, "A Monument to Southern Womanhood: The Foundation Generation of the Confederate Museum," *A Woman's War: Southern Women, Civil War and the Confederate Legacy,* Edward D.C. Campbell, Jr., ed. (Charlottesville: University of Virginia Press, 1997).

Chapter Thirteen
Virginia and the New South

Various centennials in the 1870s and 1880s—the hundred year anniversaries of George Washington assuming command of the Continental Army and the surrender at Yorktown among others—served to remind the rest of the nation of the leading role Virginia had once played in national affairs. The departure of federal troops and the Virginia General Assembly's acceptance of the Fourteenth and Fifteenth Amendments meant Reconstruction was at an end in the Commonwealth. Moreover, the relative stability of the state encouraged Northern investment.

Among the first successes was the development of coal mining in southwestern Virginia where rich deposits were uncovered. Other investors undertook railroad construction throughout the state. Indeed, it was a railroad magnate, Collis I. Huntington, who made one of the most significant contributions to reviving the state's economy, founding the Newport News Shipbuilding and Dry Dock Company, an enterprise that would make that city into one of the nation's leading shipbuilding centers.

Other small businesses sprang up. One example is the Hopkins Candy Factory, opened in 1908 in Manassas. Later, its brick building served as a grain mill. Today, it has been converted into an art center.

The race question remained, dividing white from black. A Virginian, Booker T. Washington, offered views and leadership that went far in reassuring white populations on both sides of the Mason-Dixon. While never arguing for social equality,

Washington insisted both races working side by side were "essential to mutual progress."[1] Born a slave, Washington had worked his way through Hampton Institute, rising to national prominence, founding the Tuskegee Institute in Alabama. There he fashioned a curriculum designed to provide blacks with the skills necessary to secure work in various trades. Only after achieving some economic security, Washington believed, could future generations of black children find the luxury to pursue more classical education. "The opportunity to earn a dollar in a factory is worth infinitely more than the opportunity to spend a dollar in an opera house."[2]

This seeming willingness on the part of blacks to accept "their place," that is, second-class citizenship for the foreseeable future, reassured Northerners who invested money in Washington's plans for black education. President Theodore Roosevelt went even further, making Washington his advisor on race questions, particularly those involving the appointment of black officials to federal positions.

Yet Virginians did not meet the good will Washington sought to foster, nor did any of the other Southern states, once whites reclaimed political power. Lacking the economic equality to protect the political liberty guaranteed to them by the Fourteenth and Fifteenth Amendments, many blacks fell back on sharecropping, fighting the inevitable downward spiral into poverty that was the fate of tenant farmers. Although no longer slaves in name, they were still tied to the soil and subservient to the power of white landowners.

In Virginia, as elsewhere, the legislature enacted Jim Crow laws to keep blacks from voting, a tactic designed to make the Democratic Party supreme in the South by ensuring those still loyal to the party of Lincoln did not venture near a voting booth. The Jim Crow era went further, strictly segregating the races in all public places including schools, restaurants, public transportation, etc. "Separate but equal," facilities became the law, if not the reality. There was little equality in the education provided for blacks. And after D. W. Griffith's 1915 film, *The Birth of a Nation*, revived the Ku Klux Klan, the General Assembly passed anti-lynching laws. Still, in Virginia, most of the worst excesses of the era were avoided.

There was some violence in Virginia directed against blacks but, for the most part, state officials resisted mob efforts to seize black prisoners. Moreover, several prominent Virginians openly challenged the doctrine of "white supremacy" accepted elsewhere in the nation. Instead, Virginians concentrated on supporting black education at St. Paul's Normal and Industrial Institute, today St. Paul's College, an Episcopal center of higher learning in Lawrenceville. The Baptists followed suit, organizing Virginia Union University in Richmond in 1899. Other predominantly black universities are discussed in chapter 8.

The series of economic depressions the country suffered in 1870s, '80s, and '90s hit Virginia hard. Tobacco production fell in those decades, producing stark poverty, particularly in the region of the Southside, where farmers had clung to their dependence on this single cash crop. By contrast, the Tidewater area expanded into truck farming and peanut cultivation. Virginians living along the Chesapeake Bay looked to the sea for their livelihoods, developing commercial fishing operations. In the Piedmont, dairy farming became the most common means of making a living, particularly in counties like Nottaway in central Virginia.[3] Like their neighbors in North Carolina, Virginians began harvesting their rich timber resources, although much of the lumber was shipped out of state to the furniture factories in North Carolina. With more foresight, Virginians did develop facilities for cigarette manufacturing, beginning in 1873 with the formation of P. H. May and Bros. Tobacco Company in Richmond. At the end of World War I, Phillip Morris also made its base in Richmond.

What is striking about the industrial development of the New South is the degree to which it was still based around the

A 1919 photograph of a black sharecropper tending his tobacco crop in the shadow of a memorial to Robert E. Lee on Richmond's Monument Avenue.

Sir Moses Ezakiel's bronze statue of Lieutenant General Thomas Jonathan "Stonewall" Jackson, located on the west side of the cadet barracks of the Virginia Military Institute, where he instructed cadets before the Civil War. General Jackson is depicted surveying his army at the Battle of Chancellorsville, on May 2, 1863, the day of his greatest triumph and also of the wound that proved to be fatal. His words to his cavalry leader, Colonel Thomas T. Munford, are inscribed upon the base of the statue: "The Institute will be heard from today."

CREDIT: Claire Clauss

concept of "cash crops"—lumber, tobacco, and cotton. This ensured that the state would remain largely rural with few cities of any size. And, as always, Virginia pursued its love of horses. The raising of purebred steeds became very profitable in the northern Piedmont, especially in Loudon County.

But the vision of University of Virginia professor Noah K. Davis proved correct. In 1886, he had published an article on race relations, writing, "Color is nonessential . . . The time may come when a Negro shall be our Secretary of State; and who will be foolish enough to object? . . . Brains, not color, must settle rank."[4] Indeed, it would be the black populations of Virginia who would contribute more at the turn of the twentieth century than any other group.

One of the best examples is that of Maggie L. Walker, a black businesswoman who chartered St. Luke Penny Savings Bank in 1903, and the first woman bank president in America. Another Richmond woman, Dorothy Height, spent a lifetime fighting for civil rights, serving as president of the National Council of Negro Women for over forty years.[5] Even more, it was black Virginians who made truly significant contributions in education. Buckingham County resident Carter G. Woodson founded the *Journal of Negro History* and wrote more than a dozen books on black history. Charles S. Johnson of Bristol founded the journal *Opportunity*, and later became president of Fisk University. P. B. Young founded Norfolk's *Journal and Guide*, and was its editor. Other black Virginia authors include Ambrose Caliver, Abram L. Harris, and Ira DeA. Reid.

Black Virginians also made notable achievements in the arts, including Richmond sculptor Leslie G. Bolling and the painter George H. Ben Johnson, also a native of Richmond. Yet another Richmonder, Charles S. Gilpin, achieved notable success as an actor. Dorothy Maynor of Norfolk, Virginia was praised for her voice by the director of the Boston Symphony.

Danville native Camilla Williams became a leading soprano with the New York City Opera Company. Dr. Paul Freeman continued their legacy, making his own contributions to the arts as a musician. In 1970, he was appointed conductor of the Detroit Symphony.[6]

These Virginians exhibited so much talent, yet they had to travel elsewhere to pursue and develop it—Maynor to Boston, Williams to New York, and Freeman to Detroit. The doctrine of "separate but equal" drove some of the best of Virginia's young people away to seek their success elsewhere in the country.

Even some white Virginians sought their fame elsewhere, notably Willa Cather, born in Winchester. One of the South's best-known historians, Douglas Southall Freeman, hailed from Virginia, as did his fellow Richmond authors, Ellen Glasgow and James Branch Cabell, all of whom rose to international fame in the 1930s. Freeman, in particular, enjoyed public notoriety and was a tireless writer, serving as editor of the Richmond *News-Leader* for over thirty years.[7]

While some Virginians reveled in the renewal of activity in scholarship and the arts, others remained focused on redeeming Virginia's prestige and power in the nation. To achieve those ends, the Democratic Party in Virginia, as elsewhere in the South, concentrated on the United States Senate, returning men for repeated terms of office so that they could secure that vital seniority that enabled them to control Senate committees and therefore Senate business. The foremost Virginian politician of the twentieth century was Harry F. Byrd, who emerged as chairman of the state Democratic committee in 1922. First elected a state senator, he soon moved on to the governor's office and then the United States Senate where he remained for over thirty years.

By the 1930s the Byrd political machine was well established, as was the era of the "Yellow-Dog Democrat," an epitaph describing people who vowed they would rather vote for a yellow dog than a Republican. Other Southern senators who were kept in office for decades by their constituents, seeking the power Senate seniority conveyed, included Richard Russell of Georgia (serving from 1931 until 1972), John Stennis of Mississippi (1947–88), and of course the legendary Strom Thurmond of South Carolina. Conservative Democrats all, Thurmond, Russell, and Byrd would later fight to maintain segregation. The success of Franklin Roosevelt's New Deal brought the majority of Virginia's black voters into the Democratic Party, thereby creating a solid Democratic South. This political power base continued until the strife of the 1960s elevated Richard Nixon to the presidency. The Reagan revolution of the 1980s transformed Virginia into a state with a significant percentage of Republican voters.

Throughout most of the twentieth century, however, the Southern Democratic strategy of Senate control proved successful in Virginia, as elsewhere, and resulted in needed monies appropriated by Congress for various Southern projects. In Virginia most notably, Senate power resulted in the creation of a significant number of navy and army bases, still today a significant contributor to the Commonwealth's economy. In addition to the naval base at Norfolk, other military installations include Camp Pickett near Radford, Camp Lee near Petersburg, and Camp Pendleton in Virginia Beach, not to mention the Marine base at Quantico and indeed the presence of the Pentagon in northern Virginia.

The influx of federal investment did much to offset the economic calamities facing Virginians in the drought of the 1920s (which produced the Dust Bowl on the Great Plains and destroyed crops in the East) and the Great Depression that followed. But Virginians did not rely on federal largesse alone to meet these challenges. Instead, they turned to their own history, determined to restore Virginia's pride in its past. This effort marked the beginning of an extensive movement for historic preservation that set a model for the rest of the country.

Notes

1. 1895 Address at the Atlanta Exposition found in Booker T. Washington, *Up From Slavery: An Autobiography* (first published in 1907, republished by Dover Publications, 1995).
2. Ibid.
3. In recent years, this industry has fallen on hard times. As of this writing, only six dairy farms remain in the county.
4. Virginius Dabney, *Virginia: The New Dominion* (New York: Doubleday & Company, 1971), 414.
5. See Dorothy I. Heights, *Open Wide the Freedom Gates: A Memoir* (Public Affairs, 2003).
6. Dabney, 504, 535.
7. Freeman is best remembered for his studies of famous Virginians, including *R. E. Lee; Lee's Lieutenants: A Study in Command;* his multi-volume series, entitled, *Washington,* and his four-volume series, *Lee.* See also *Douglas Southall Freeman on Leadership.*

Chapter Fourteen
Preserving the Past

Virginians have long been proud of their past—their role as the first English colony in North America, their leadership in the American Revolution and the Constitutional Convention, and the power the state wielded during the first decades of the nineteenth century, when three successive Virginia presidents—Thomas Jefferson, James Madison, and James Monroe—led the country. The state's place at the heart of the Confederacy, with the Confederate capital at Richmond and the Army of Northern Virginia led by Robert E. Lee, added patina to an already well-established state pride. In the decades following the war, Virginians tried to weave their tattered dignity into whole cloth again through a crafted devotion to "The Lost Cause." In 1895, New York's formation of the American Scenic and Historic Preservation Society, a group that concentrated of saving houses of historical significance, established a new way for Virginians to celebrate their state's culture.

Actually, there had been a prewar attempt at historic preservation in Virginia when, in the 1850s, Ann Pamela Cunningham led the way in forming the Mount Vernon Ladies' Association, composed of women from each of the then thirty states. The president's home had fallen on hard times. Many of the relics from Washington's life had already been sold off to try and keep the farm going, but the house was very rundown. In 1858, Cunningham persuaded the last family owner, John Augustine Washington, Jr., a great-great-nephew of the president, to sell the plantation to the Ladies' Association. This nonprofit group set about restoring the house and gardens, working their way room by room to refurbish the home in the time period when George and Martha Washington had lived there. Work on the outbuildings and gardens continues today. In the 1940s, the association also raised the monies necessary to purchase 750 acres on the other side of the Potomac to preserve the view from Mount Vernon. This land is today part of the four-thousand-acre Piscataway National Park.

Two decades earlier, a U.S. naval officer, Uriah Phillips Levy, had bought Thomas Jefferson's beloved Monticello, which, like Mount Vernon, was suffering from neglect. Jefferson's daughter, Polly Randolph, had been forced to sell the home in 1827. The new owner, James T. Barclay, a Charlottesville druggist bought the house at public auction, proceeding to try and convert Jefferson's plantation into a silkworm farm. The ventured failed and in 1836, he sold the property to Levy.

Uriah Levy invested considerable family funds to preserve the house and grounds. Long an admirer of Jefferson, Levy (who had amassed a small fortune in New York real estate) began by commissioning a life-size bronze statue of the president for the U.S. Capitol's Rotunda. Yet his purchase of Monticello caused some upset among Virginians, in part as a response to Levy as Northerner, but perhaps equally in an expression of anti-Semitism. Levy ignored them, acquiring workers (including some new slaves he purchased) to begin much-needed repairs on the interior's ceilings and floors. He even restored Jefferson's famous pulley-operated seven-day clock that stands in the foyer.

During the Civil War, the Confederate government seized Monticello, selling it to Benjamin F. Ficklin, who lived nearby, in 1864. But at war's end, Ficklin's deed became worthless, the property reverting to the Levy family. Uriah Levy had died in 1858, his will leaving Monticello to the "people of the United States" for the purpose of establishing a farming school for the orphans of American sailors, an aim he, no doubt, saw in keeping with Jefferson's well-known faith in the yeoman farmers as well as a tribute to Levy's own career in the navy. If Congress refused to honor the bequest, Levy's last testament dictated that the estate should go to the Commonwealth of Virginia for the same educational purposes. If Virginia did not take it, Monticello would be left to the Portuguese Hebrew congregations of New York, Philadelphia, and Richmond, again on condition that it be used as a school.

Levy's heirs disputed the will, letting many years pass during which Monticello fell into near shambles. Finally in 1879, a nephew, Jefferson Monroe Levy, reached a settlement with the family by which he purchased the house and grounds for $10,500.[1]

Like his uncle, Jefferson Levy spent occasional summer months at Monticello; he never actually lived there. He did make considerable repairs, however, installing modern conveniences, including running water, toilets, and central heating. Unlike his uncle, he also took care to make friends with his Charlottesville neighbors, donating money to restore the Town Hall, renaming it the Levy Opera House, which still stands today as an office building. He also opened Monticello to tourists, charging small fees; the full proceeds of which were donated to Charlottesville charities.

Levy may have won over Virginians but he still faced a plethora of opposition from a country growing increasingly alarmed at the number of Jewish immigrants from Eastern Europe entering the nation in the late nineteenth century. Many well-known national writers began to protest a Jew's possession of the home built by the "Sage of Monticello." A write-in campaign was begun to try and force Congress to purchase the house from the "alien" Levy, who was, in fact, a fifth-generation American.[2] Levy successfully repelled efforts to wrest Monticello from him through the first two decades of the twentieth century, until his own failing finances forced him to sell at last. The signing of the deed was delayed until April 13, 1923 (Jefferson's 180th birthday), when the nonprofit group organized for the purpose, The Thomas Jefferson Foundation of Albany, New York, took control. Losing Monticello broke Levy's heart; he died three months later.

In the years that followed, the foundation has maintained control of Monticello, restoring the house and grounds to act both as a museum and an educational site for the visitors that throng to the top of Jefferson's "little mountain" each year. Approximately half of the lands that Jefferson originally owned have been purchased for inclusion as part of the site today. Visitors may see the home much as it existed when Jefferson lived there.[3] His grave lies on the property as well. Recently, that family cemetery has been the scene of some contention between the descendants of Jefferson and those of Sally Hemings, the latter of whom claim Jefferson blood.

Born to a slave mother, Elizabeth (Betty) Hemings, and very likely also the daughter of John Wayles, Thomas Jefferson's father-in-law, Sally Hemings seems to have caught Jefferson's attention because of her resemblance to his late wife, Martha. Lacking a direct male line, DNA tests alone cannot establish Jefferson's paternity of any of Sally Hemings's children. What can be proved is that a Jefferson (some claim it was Jefferson himself; others point to a nephew who frequently visited Monticello) fathered Hemings's son, Eston. Her son, Thomas, also claimed that Jefferson was his father.

While Jefferson never freed Sally Hemings, he did grant her four surviving children their liberty, an unprecedented move for a man who could not afford to manumit his remaining slaves. Like their mother, almost all of Hemings's children were light-skinned; one son, Beverly, moved to Washington where he "passed" as white. Her daughter Harriet also passed. After Jefferson's death, his daughter, Martha Randolph gave Sally Hemings "her time," a sort of unofficial freedom in keeping with the laws of the state during that era. Direct manumission would have made Hemings subject to the state requirement of the 1820s that free blacks leave in one year. Instead, Sally Hemings lived with her sons, Thomas and Eston, in Charlottesville for the remainder of her life (she died in 1835).

Eston was so sure of Jefferson's paternity that he changed his name from Hemings to Jefferson after he moved to Wisconsin in 1852. Rumors of the controversy had circulated even in Jefferson's lifetime, used as fodder by his political enemies, and in the late twentieth century, the scientific journal, *Nature*, revived and addressed them, publishing a report on the DNA tests. In reaction, the Thomas Jefferson Foundation commissioned its own investigation. DNA taken from blood samples at the University of Virginia was sent to Oxford in 2000 and tested by three laboratories. The conclusion indicates that Thomas Jefferson was almost certainly the father of Eston and that he possibly sired all six of Hemings's children, although more recent studies have cast doubt over that second claim.[4]

Today, the many descendants of Thomas Jefferson are divided, sometimes bitterly, over whether Hemings' heirs should be permitted burial in the family plot at Monticello. At the annual family reunions, the efforts of both sides of the family to reach reconciliation make front-page news throughout Virginia.

Monticello and its grounds are truly breathtaking in their beauty. The estate also boasts the distinction of being the only house in America designated by the United Nations as part of the World's Heritage List of sites that must be protected.

The concept of saving historic homes as house museums, established at Mount Vernon and Monticello, made an important contribution to the preservation movement in the United States. Henry Ford added a new twist in his creation of the museum village at Dearborn, Michigan, where he collected historical artifacts in what he called, "Greenfield Village," adjacent to Menlo Park and the laboratories of Thomas Edison, America's genius inventor. Nearby are the homes of American composer Stephen Foster; the author of America's first dictionary, Noah Webster; and the bicycle shop of Wilbur and Orville Wright. Preserving all of the structures together in a museum-like setting, Ford established a precedent that would be quickly followed, most famously by John D. Rockefeller, Jr., in his reconstruction of Colonial Williamsburg, beginning in the 1920s.

Like Monticello, Virginia's best-known tourist attraction, Williamsburg, was initially restored by New York money. Heir to the Standard Oil fortune amassed by his father, Rockefeller devoted himself to preserving those few surviving Williamsburg buildings that predated 1790. Using colonial records and even going to the extraordinary lengths of ordering his craftsmen to utilize the same tools and materials that would have been available to eighteenth-century builders, Rockefeller reconstructed Williamsburg as it had appeared at the time of the American Revolution. He sent salvaging teams throughout the state to try to recover eighteenth century artifacts. One result of these scavenging expeditions was the disappearance of doorknobs from many of Virginia's plantation homes. Virginians had never recovered any semblance of economic prosperity in the decades following the Civil War. The droughts of the 1920s had worsened an already precarious existence for many of these families who therefore had no choice but to sell what they had to Rockefeller in the 1920s and 1930s. Ornately carved mantles, many of them crafted by slave labor, were taken as well, but it is the absence of those doorknobs that remains most noticeable. As restoration continues on some of Virginia's plantation homes today, one is struck by the rags placed in those holes left by the missing doorknobs, both to cut down on drafts and to open and close the doors.

Williamsburg proved to be a phenomenal success. Today visitors may wander from the Capitol to the Governor's Mansion, visiting Bruton Parish Church and enjoying a meal in Raleigh's Tavern, where the Rump Session of the House of Burgesses gathered in 1774 to call for the meeting of the First Continental Congress. Many examples of colonial craft-making and simple day-to-day life abound, all reenacted by men and women outfitted in period dress. More than five hundred restored and reconstructed buildings stretching over three hundred acres, staffed by thirty-five hundred archeologists, historians, and guides, make Colonial Williamsburg the world's largest historic museum. Close by is the site of the Jamestown Settlement and the Yorktown Victory Center, visited by thousands annually.

The success of Rockefeller's patriotic village dream prompted the development of other museum villages throughout the nation, particularly in the East at Old Sturbridge Village and Plymouth Village, both located in Massachusetts. In Virginia, Williamsburg called new attention to the wealth of the state's history and spurred the Commonwealth to new endeavors to protect its past. Richmond's historic Fan district, home to a plethora of houses, survived the Revolutionary War, only to be nearly lost in the fire of 1865. Extensive rebuilding began in the 1920s and the Fan is today a National Register District. The Executive Mansion, the oldest continually occupied governor's residence in the United States, is now a National Historic Landmark. Richmond can also lay claim to the largest National Historic Landmark district in the country. Jackson Ward spans forty blocks, an African-American neighborhood once set off by what was called the Black Wall in the 1880s. Home to Bill "Bojangles" Robinson and Maggie Walker among others, the district's inventory today identifies more than six hundred structures of historical significance.

The creation of the National Trust for Historic Preservation in 1949, with the subsequent Historic Preservation Act in 1966, provided federal incentives to make preservation profitable and

The Wickham House on East Clay Street in the Fan District. Designed by American architect Robert Mills, and constructed in 1812 for noted Richmond attorney John Wickham, it is maintained today by the Valentine Museum as an outstanding example of Federalist architecture and furniture.
CREDIT: Kathren Barnes

therefore much more likely. The creation of the National Park Service and its assumption of responsibility for national military parks aided in the preservation of a host of Civil War battle sites throughout Virginia at Appomattox, Fredericksburg and Spotsylvania, Cold Harbor, Petersburg, Manassas, the Wilderness Battlefield, and Richmond National Battlefield Park. Other battlefields designated as state sites include Saylor's Creek, scene of the last battle leading to the surrender at Appomattox, just east of Farmville, and New Market Battlefield State Historic Park.

*The John Marshall House. Built in 1799, it is now home to the
Chief Justice of the United States Supreme Court.*

Private monies were used as well. In 1954, the Stonewall Jackson Foundation purchased the general's home in Lexington, restoring it to its 1860 appearance. It is open to the public with guided tours provided daily. Lexington was also the birthplace of Sam Houston, at a spot marked today by a thirty-eight thousand-pound Texas pink granite monument.

The Association for the Preservation of Virginia Antiquities, founded in 1889, today maintains thirty-four historic properties, including the John Marshall house in Richmond. Built in 1799 and home for forty-five years to the nation's first chief justice, the house provides a splendid example of Federalist architecture. Visitors may tour it as well as hundreds of other sites dotted throughout the state.

In the Tidewater region, tourists often begin with Bacon's Castle in Surrey. Constructed in 1665 by Arthur Allen, it remains one of the oldest brick homes still standing in English North America. It may be viewed as part of the Virginia Plantation Country tour that takes groups to six sites.

Berkeley Plantation is perhaps the most famous of the "houses that tobacco built." Constructed in 1726, this Georgian mansion and its extensive grounds lie in Charles County.

William Byrd II's Westover Plantation, finished in 1730, provides another splendid example of Georgian architecture and the wealth enjoyed by some Virginia planters, those few elites of the ruling oligarchy in the eighteenth century.

Visitors to northern Virginia are familiar with the Custis-Lee Mansion that lies on the hilltop overlooking Arlington Cemetery. Nearby stands George Mason's Gunston Hall Plantation, a brick mansion dating from 1799 and home to the author of the state's Bill of Rights. Moving southward to Fredericksburg, tourists may visit the Mary Washington House, purchased in 1772 by George Washington for his mother. Rescued from demolition by a group of determined Fredericksburg women, the home today is operated by the Association for the Preservation of Virginia Antiquities.

Student re-enactors celebrating colonial culture at Henrico, Va., the second Virginian settlement, after Jamestown.

CREDIT TOP: Andrei Tehernov (www.istock.com)
BOTTOM: Galina Dreytlna (www.istock.com)

To the west lies Patrick Henry's final and favorite home, Red Hill, the small plantation he called "one of the garden spots of the world."[5] His grave is on the estate. Near Charlottesville, one may visit Ash Lawn-Highland, completed in 1799 as the home of James Monroe, fifth president of the United States. In Staunton, a short distance away, the birthplaces of President Woodrow Wilson and inventor Cyrus McCormick may be toured. Moving into the Western Highlands, other historic sites abound ranging from the birthplace of singer/comedian Tennessee Ernie Ford in Bristol to the Andrew Johnston House in Pearlsburg.

Museum sites celebrating Virginia's past abound throughout the Commonwealth. One of the most famous is the White House of the Confederacy in Richmond, home to Jefferson Davis throughout the war years. Over 50 percent of the furnishings of the Davis family are still in place. More significantly, the surrounding museum houses the world's largest collection of artifacts and documents connected to the Civil War period. Chartered on May 31, 1890 (Memorial Day) as the Confederate Memorial Literary Society, the museum opened to the public in 1896.

In many cities and towns—not just the captured but Petersburg, Tazewell, Newport News, and elsewhere—whole districts have been set aside, protected for their historical significance. One of the lesser-known but interesting spots is the town of Stanardsville, in the foothills, on the old stagecoach road taken by nineteenth century travelers seeking cooler mountain air during the hot summer months. In the center of town lies the Lafayette Hotel, privately owned by individuals committed to its restoration. Significantly, intact slave quarters still exist on land adjacent to the property. Most slave housing was so shabbily constructed that it could not survive into modern times. The hotel's separate building, providing accommodations for servants traveling with their owners, was constructed of brick and so remains, a rare relic of those years.

Entrance to the Little White House, where Jefferson Davis lived during the Civil War until Richmond was evacuated in 1865.
CREDIT: Kathren Barnes

One of the best examples of local initiative being devoted to preservation can be found in Emporia, Virginia, about an hour south of Richmond. There, town residents came together to save the Village View Mansion House. Built in the 1790s for James Wall, the house has been home to the Wall, Land, and Briggs families. Most famously, its front parlor served as the site of a meeting between generals W. H. F. Lee, Wade Hampton, and Matthew Butler as they planned their defense of Petersburg. After the war, the house, as well as its many outbuildings, became a doctor's office, an apothecary and briefly a boy's academy. Over the last decades, residents of Emporia have joined together to rescue the mansion from ruin. Lovingly restored (although still missing many of its doorknobs, which were taken for use in the Williamsburg construction), the house is open to tours today and is well worth the stop, both to see a federalist era plantation and to meet the splendid people who are working to preserve it.

Perhaps the most famous restoration project ongoing in present-day Virginia is at Montpelier, the home of James Madison, the fourth president of the United States. Located not far from Jefferson's Monticello and Monroe's Ash Lawn, Montpelier was first constructed in 1732 by Ambrose Madison. His grandson, James, would add significantly to the house, creating a mansion of twenty-two rooms. After his death, the property changed hands many times. In 1901, William duPont bought it and altered it in almost every detail, including tearing out staircases and walls, as well as building new additions that doubled the size of the house. His daughter, Marion, inherited the estate in 1928. It was she who added the horse tracks, one for steeplechasing and one flat track. The area is still famous for its horses.

Marion duPont Scott willed the property to the National Trust for Historic Preservation at her death in 1983. Today,

A Winter scene at Village View Mansion House, a Federalist era mansion in Emporia, VA.

The first floor hallway of the Village View House. Built in the 1790s, the house is now restored and open for public tours by the community. The plans for the defense of Petersburg were drawn in the front parlor.

under the stewardship of the Montpelier Foundation, significant renovation work is underway to remove the duPont additions and restore the home to the way it looked when James and Dolly Madison lived there in the early nineteenth century. This vast undertaking, involving considerable archeological and historical expertise, has so far been successful in locating the original walls and doorframes. A museum built on the property will house the duPont additions, many of which possess historical value in their own right.

It is difficult today to travel anywhere in Virginia and not come across a site of historical significance. From the birthplace of Booker T. Washington to that of Benjamin Harrison, from the early settlement at Jamestown to the site of Lee's surrender at Appomattox, from the Chesapeake to the Cumberland Gap, Virginia abounds in history and natural beauty. As a result, tourism became a major industry in Virginia during the twentieth century. To capitalize on that new industry, the state decided to take advantage of its scenic countryside.

Notes

1. For a complete account of the Levy contribution to saving Monticello, see Charles B. Hosmer, Jr., *Presence of the Past: A History of the Preservation Movement in the United States before Williamsburg* (Washington: National Trust for Historic Preservation, 1965) and Merrill D. Peterson, *Jefferson Image in the American Mind* (New York: Oxford University Press, 1992). Interested readers may also wish to consult the Thomas Jefferson Foundation's Web page at www.monticello.org.
2. See Patricia West, *Domesticating History: The Political Origins of America's House Museums* (Washington: Smithsonian Institution Press, 1999).

3. Those unable to visit Monticello are encouraged to visit the Foundation's Web site (see above). There one may click on various links to take a visual tour of the mansion and grounds.

4. For a full account of the Jefferson-Hemings controversy, see Joseph Ellis, *American Sphinx, The Character of Thomas Jefferson* (New York: Knopf, 1997) and an even more passionate argument in Annette Gordon-Reid's *Thomas Jefferson and Sally Hemings, An American Controversy* (Charlottesville: University of Virginia Press, 1998).

5. To view Red Hill, please visit their Web site at www.redhill.org. For a tour of many of Virginia's historic homes, districts, and museums, please consult the following site: www.virginia.org.

Chapter Fifteen
Scenic Wonders

Virginians had long been aware of the beauty of their coastline and rare natural wonders such as Natural Bridge in the western part of the state. In the 1870s, they began to record the locations of magnificent caverns, most of them lying beneath the Shenandoah Valley. The most famous is Luray, discovered by a tinsmith and a local photographer in 1878. The Luray Caverns are enormous, with cathedral-sized rooms, some of them ten stories high. The following year near New Market, two boys out hunting chased a rabbit down a hole. Pulling stones aside to pursue, they stumbled across a series of caves now known as Endless Caverns. To date, five miles of caves have been mapped and the exploration continues.

The marvelous mineral formations, clear pools, and breathtaking beauty of these underground wonders would obviously have drawn tourists if only a way could have been found for them to reach the backcountry of the state. By the early twentieth century, Americans had fallen in love with the automobile, and large-scale road construction had started nationwide. In Virginia, Congress proposed construction of the Skyline Drive as a route to a presidential retreat. The work began in 1929 and was later finished as one of the projects of the New Deal's Civilian Conservation Corps to enable tourists to drive the Blue Ridge Parkway from Front Royal, Virginia to near Cherokee, North Carolina. The 105-mile-long Skyline Drive crests the top of the mountains, enabling travelers to take in magnificent scenic views. It also provided access to the caverns. Shenandoah Caverns was open to the public in 1922.[1] Skyline

Natural Bridge in the Shenandoah Valley, one of the most famous natural wonders of Virginia. Geologists speculate that erosion created this natural rock formation. Natural Bridge and Niagara Falls were the major tourist attractions for visiting Europeans in the 18th and 19th centuries.

In the 1750s George Washington surveyed Natural Bridge and carved his initials into the rock. The letters are still visible today. Thomas Jefferson bought the Bridge for 20 shillings in 1774, and built a cabin nearby as a retreat.

Caverns was opened as well. The latter is particularly famous for its Anthodites—"Orchids of the Mineral Kingdom." They seem to almost float in the air, making the whole experience like wandering through a fairy land.

In 1926, President Calvin Coolidge authorized the creation of Shenandoah National Park, designating a half million acres for its use—with one codicil typical of Coolidge: no federal funds could be used. Anxious to promote tourism, Virginians initiated a "Buy an acre for $6.60" campaign which proved remarkably successful. On December 26, 1935, the state presented the federal government with over 175,000 acres and in the following July, Shenandoah National Park became a reality, with President Franklin Delano Roosevelt presiding over the dedication.

The only problem lay with the many families who had lived in the Valley for generations and did not want to move. In the middle of the Depression few had anywhere to go, and many did not wish to relinquish their lands. Under the New Deal, Congress voted to help families relocate despite the opposition of conservative senators like Harry Byrd. Some families, sensing this was not a battle they could win, accepted the aid, and a few even enjoyed their new homes, which had running water and other amenities their mountain shacks had lacked. Those who held on were removed by force, often standing by in tears as they watched the only homes they had ever known burned or torn down.

The Shenandoah National Park has provided millions of people with access to some of the most beautiful country in the state, rich in wildlife and a glorious wilderness of cold mountain creeks and waterfalls. But the land was achieved at a high price for those who lived there. The park offers more than five hundred miles of trails, including one hundred miles of the Appalachian Trail. In trekking through that country, one often comes across apple orchards, stone foundations, and family cemeteries—all reminders of the people who were compelled to leave. As along Skyline Drive, much of the work in the Shenandoah National Park was undertaken by the Civilian Conservation Corps, who arrived 1933, and began creating trails and building access roads.

About a quarter of the entire Appalachian Trail lies in Virginia, running more or less parallel to the Blue Ridge Parkway. Opened in 1937, the trail was designated as the first National Scenic Trail by the 1968 National Trails System Act. Stretching through fourteen states from Maine to Georgia, it is over two thousand miles in length.

In 1956, an equally ambitious undertaking was begun on the other side of the state. Ferry traffic had become so crowded in the Chesapeake Bay that the General Assembly appointed first the Chesapeake Bay Ferry Commission and later the Chesapeake Bay Bridge and Tunnel District and Commission. Their charge: to explore options to construct a fixed crossing. Over $200 million was raised in bonds for the project; no federal funds were used. Opened on April 15, 1964, the Chesapeake Bay, Bridge Tunnel stretches approximately seventeen and a half miles over and under the Chesapeake Bay connecting southeastern Virginia with the Delmarva Peninsula (Delaware plus counties in Maryland and Virginia's Eastern Shore). Still considered a modern engineering wonder, the bridge is used by commuters and tourists alike.

Equally important to Virginia economic development in the twentieth century was the system of interstate highways built to crisscross the state. The concept of connecting the nation through a network of wide roads had first been discussed in the 1930s with a model six-lane highway shown at the 1939 New York World's Fair. Squelched by New Deal opponents and then the nation's preoccupation with World War II and then Korea, the project was put on hold until Dwight D. Eisenhower took office. Eisenhower had witnessed the benefits of the German autobahn system during the war. Moreover, he saw the interstate highways as a way to unite America's regions.

Considerable Congressional opposition had to be over-come. Harry F. Byrd of Virginia led those who objected to the large public debt that the project would incur. Other Southern Congressional leaders disagreed. Senator Albert Gore, Sr., of Tennessee and Representative Hale Boggs of Louisiana played pivotal roles in introducing legislation that employed various means (including raising the gas tax from two to three cents per gallon) that would render construction fiscally feasible.

Congress passed the Federal-Aid Highway Act in 1956. This legislation led to the onset of construction of two significant interstate highways that traverse Virginia north to south—Interstate 81 in the west (in the Roanoke region) and Interstate 95 in the east, providing easy access from the District of Columbia south to Richmond and on into North Carolina. It was left to the state to construct necessary east–west thorough-fares, including Highways 360 and 460.

Throughout this period of major developments in trans-portation and the opening of some of Virginia's most pristine lands to visitors from both within state and without, the Com-monwealth's politics continued to be dominated by a single man—Harry F. Byrd. A descendent of the Byrds of Westover Plantation, Harry Byrd entered the Virginia state senate in 1916 when he was only twenty-eight. In 1926, he became governor. A noted fiscal conservative (a political viewpoint he would manifest more strongly in later years), Byrd nonetheless believed in progress. He combined both views by streamlining state government, eliminating many positions. He also asked the General Assembly for large appropriations to support road construction, education, and hospitals while at the same time reorganizing the tax structure with an eye to attracting industry to the Commonwealth. The latter effort achieved spectacular results, enabling Byrd to claim that in "fiscal year

1927 Virginia made the largest industrial progress of any state in the Union."[2] No idle boast—over $250,000,000 manufacturing capital was added in this single year.

Yet Byrd was a solid Democrat, no admirer of President Coolidge's hands-off policy when it came to American business. He fought both gasoline and telephone companies to secure lower rates for Virginia. That sort of tenacity plus the fiscal efficiency he brought to state management turned the deficit he had inherited into a surplus of over $4,000,000 by the time he left office.

Ironically, Byrd, a well-known champion of the Anti-Saloon League, served as governor during the era of Prohibition while one of the major cottage industries in the state was moonshining. Called Poteen (Irish for "The Water of Life") or Mountain Dew, the brews—usually corn liquor, dripping out of homemade stills and sold in mason jars among the local populace—kept many a family afloat during the hard times of the 1920s. Remnants of rusty tubing and charred stone circles can still be found along many streams throughout Virginia, evidence of the widespread production of illicit whiskey that kept "Revenuers" busy.

During the Prohibition Era, Virginians may have bought their liquor quietly from a nearby farmer, but publicly they espoused respectable "dry" principles. The nomination of Al Smith as the Democratic candidate for president in 1928 sorely tested Virginia's opposition to the party of Lincoln. Smith not only favored an end to Prohibition; he was a Catholic as well, the first ever nominated to be president. Anti-Catholicism had never been particularly pronounced in Virginia, but enough of it existed to enable the Republican candidate, Herbert Hoover, to carry the state in the election.

This anomaly did not mark any real change in the state's determination to remain part of the solid Democratic South. Those who voted for Hoover quickly returned to the party fold, voting straight tickets henceforth. That included sending Harry F. Byrd to the United States Senate where he would serve for thirty-two years.

The Great Depression of the 1930s struck hard in Virginia. Already hurt by the droughts of the 1920s, tobacco farmers watched as prices continued to drop throughout the 1930s. Mills closed; the mines in the southwestern part of the state were forced to shut down; banks began to fail—scenes repeated throughout the country.

Senator Byrd, an enthusiastic supporter of Franklin D. Roosevelt at the onset, voted for many of the New Deal Programs that would bring some relief (at least employment for its young men) to Virginia—the CCC and the WPA. The latter also resulted in a number of state historical records being collected. The State Writers' Project produced *Virginia: A Guide to the Old Dominion*.[3] The Federal Emergency Relief Act and the Tennessee Valley Authority both brought needed funds to Virginia, the former in direct cash. The latter only touched the southwestern edge of the state. The Rural Electrification Administration brought electricity to southern and western Virginians, resulting in the formation of cooperative organizations by farmers anxious both to extend the electrical lines and lower the rates for their usage.[4]

The Agricultural Adjustment Act passed despite Senator Byrd's opposition and generally received the endorsement of Virginia's farmers. So many were already dirt poor, many of them tenant farmers; these people had little to lose. But at least they could grow their own food, as did many people throughout rural Virginia. In many ways the state fared better during this period than Northern cities did. But for Virginia, as the rest of the nation, the Depression only came to an end with America's entry into the Second World War.

Notes

1. All of the caverns are chilly, holding a steady temperature of around 56º Fahrenheit. Elevators have been installed in the Shenandoah Caverns for those who need them.
2. Virginius Dabney, *Virginia: The New Dominion* (New York: Doubleday and Company, 1971), 483.
3. Virginia Writers' Project, *Virginia: A Guide to the Old Dominion* (New York: Oxford University Press, 1940). Part of the American Guide Series, this book contains a community-by-community list of every monument and historic site in the area.
4. See "Farm Power Co-op Asks for Charter," *Richmond Times Dispatch*, September 22, 1937. Numerous articles about the farmers' demands for electrical services can be found throughout 1937–38.

Chapter Sixteen
Moving Forward

World War I brought about significant expansion of the ship-building industry in Hampton Roads area. Two decades later, while America watched World War II raging abroad, activity at the Norfolk Naval Base shifted into high gear as the United States began to prepare again for war. Radford was chosen as the site of a large munitions plant, bringing in two hundred thousand workers. Camp Pickett near Blackstone went on alert, training new recruits. Other bases were reactivated and new ones built, including Camp Peary near Williamsburg, for the Seabees who played a significant role in building airfields in the Pacific. The army began holding maneuvers at Camp A.P. Hill even as the Marines undertook the training of men at Quantico.

Nearby, the War Department began consolidation of its operations in an enormous structure on the banks of the Potomac in northern Virginia. The Pentagon was opened on January 15, 1943, bringing people from all around the nation to staff its offices. Considered an architectural marvel, the Pentagon is a vast military complex containing over seventeen miles of corridors. Yet, because of its design, it is possible to walk between any two offices in seven minutes at most.

The explosion of northern Virginia's population during World War II continues today. The Pentagon alone employs twenty-three thousand people. The burgeoning federal government of Washington D.C. has brought hundreds of thousands of others to northern Virginia.

In World War II's time of emergency, Virginia contributed many of her sons to the conflict. Army General George C. Marshall, later author of the Marshall Plan for European recovery, had been born in Pennsylvania but he made his home in Virginia. An avid horseman, he built his mansion, Dodona, near Leesburg, which is the site of the George C. Marshall International Center today. According to legend, he was riding at Dodona on that Sunday morning in December 1941 as his aides scrambled to find him after receiving intelligence indicating the Japanese were preparing to attack. Another Virginia Military Institute graduate, Lieutenant General Leonard T. Gerow of Petersburg, commanded the Omaha Beach landings at D-Day while his fellow alumnus, Lieutenant General Lewis B. Puller, of West Point, Virginia achieved distinction (five navy crosses) fighting in the Pacific. But it was the average men and women, the famous "citizen soldiers" of World War II, who bore the brunt of the fighting, and their families who often suffered their loss.

Virginians, both black and white (and red, for that matter), all shared in the sacrifices necessary to win that war. Yet returning "colored" soldiers came home to find that they were still second-class citizens in a segregated society.[1] On public transportation, in all public facilities, even in churches, "separate but equal" remained law. In education, that disparity was felt most egregiously. Black citizens were charged property taxes for the support of public education at a rate precisely the same as their white neighbors, but black families saw their children consigned to rundown buildings staffed by inferior teachers using outdated texts.

In April 1951, led by a courageous young student, sixteen-year-old Barbara Johns, niece of the civil rights leader Reverend Vernon Johns, the black students at the Robert R. Moton School in Farmville, Virginia staged a unanimous walkout in protest of conditions there. The Moton School, first constructed in

The Bedford D-Day Memorial: located in southwest Virginia, the memorial was dedicated on June 6th, 2001, the 57th anniversary of the Normandy invasion. Bedford suffered more fatalities per capita at Normandy than any other community in the United States. The Memorial consists of three distinct plazas that tell the story of D-Day: the activities leading to the D-Day order, the landing and fighting stage of the invasion, and at the third plaza—victory.

While at Victory Plaza, visitors view the Overlord Arch, the twelve Allied flags, the names of the five invasion beaches carved in black granite, the statue "The Final Tribute."

CREDIT: Kathren Barnes

In the middle plaza, visitors encounter the invasion pool with obstacles in the water—sculptures, by artist Jim Brothers, depicting soldiers struggling ashore, and a representation of the Higgins craft used for the invasion. Gunfire is replicated by jets of water rising from the pool.

CREDIT: Kathren Barnes

The *"Scaling the Wall"* sculpture in the middle plaza pays tribute to selfless teamwork as exhibited by troops on D-Day. Statuary pieces at the Memorial are known for their attention to detail and emotional expressiveness, exemplifying the virtues of valor, fidelity, and sacrifice.

CREDIT: Kathren Barnes

The "The Final Tribute," sculpted by artist Matt Kirby.
CREDIT: Kathren Barnes

1939 as a high school for African-American children in Prince Edward County, was inadequately designed from the outset. Built to hold 180 students, the school opened with 167 in its first year. By 1950, enrollment had grown to 450, and vastly overcrowded conditions resulted. In response, the county constructed temporary wooden buildings which were tar paper shacks with no insulation and often leaky roofs. Even school buses were pressed into use as classrooms.

Drawing their principal away with a phone call summoning him downtown, the students assembled in the auditorium and began their walkout—all of them, in an attempt to compel the county to offer equal education. One month later, African-American parents, joined by the NAACP, filed a suit (*Davis v. County School Board of Prince Edward County*) asking for full desegregation. That case, bundled with four others, became part of *Brown v. Board of Education*, the case in which the 1954 Supreme Court ruled that racial segregation was inherently unequal and therefore unconstitutional.[2] The following year in its *Brown II* decision, the Court ordered Prince Edward, along with the four other school boards in the Brown suit, to desegregate its public schools "with all deliberate speed."[3]

The county delayed and finally, in 1959, closed all of its schools rather than integrate. This policy was copied throughout the South as a posture of "Massive Resistance" was assumed. Private schools opened for those white students whose parents could afford the tuition. A generation was condemned to poverty by the education denied them in this era. In other cases, families divided as parents sent their children to relatives in other states so that they might achieve their diplomas.

Prince Edward County held out the longest, keeping its schools closed from 1959 until 1964, opening them again only with Court intervention provoked by black parents' demands.[4] In a 1963 speech, President Kennedy observed that "there are

An antique piece of farm equipment, one of a variety often seen abandoned in fields throughout Virginia. Some date before the 20th century, and many were left behind by farmers migrating to find work during the 1920's drought.

CREDIT: Kathren Barnes

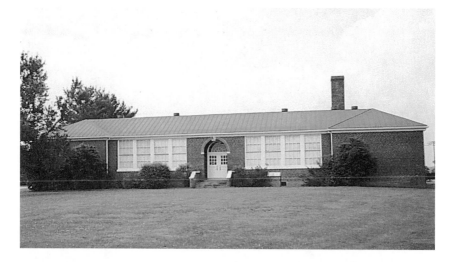

The Robert R. Moton School in Farmville, Va., the site of a1951 walkout by African-American students protesting grossly inadequate conditions. The walkout later became part of the Brown v. Board of Education ruling overturning segregation.
CREDIT: Deborah Welch

only four places in the world where children are denied the right to attend school: North Vietnam, Cambodia, North Korea, and Prince Edward County." That year, the Ford Foundation and other contributors supplied the funds necessary to open a "Free School" in the Moton building. Robert F. Kennedy even organized a "penny drive" among schoolchildren nationwide, the proceeds to be used to hire teachers to teach in the "Free School."

In an effort reminiscent of the women of Fredericksburg coming together to save the Mary Washington house, the Martha E. Forrester Council, a black ladies' association in Farmville, led the way in the 1980s to purchase and restore the Moton School building. In 1998, the school was awarded

A Commemorative Plaque on the grounds of Moton School.
CREDIT: Deborah Welch

National Historic Landmark status. Today it serves as a museum of those years when integration was hard-won. At present, plans are going forward for the creation of Civil Rights in Education Heritage Trail that would provide markers for many significant sites throughout Virginia, with the Robert R. Moton School at its center.[5]

Despite these events in Prince Edward County, the state was spared the violence that marred so much of the last half of the twentieth century as African-Americans sought their civil rights. The church bombings, riots, murders and other violence that soiled this nation's history did not occur in Virginia. In the 1950s and '60s, blacks and whites struggled against each other over the question of school integration, but as the late Reverend L. Francis Griffith, a black community leader in those years, is purported to have observed (somewhat magnanimously), "This is an argument between gentlemen. It will be settled in the courts." The street that runs beside Moton School today bears his name—Griffith Boulevard.

At present, blacks sit alongside whites on the Farmville Town Council and on the Prince Edward County Board of Supervisors. Is racism dead? Of course not—not in Virginia, nor anywhere else in the country. Still, Virginia has tried. In 1990, Richmond attorney L. Douglas Wilder was elected governor of the Commonwealth, the first African-American to achieve the governorship of any state in the Union. Although limited by state constitution to one term, Doug Wilder remains an active force in Virginia politics—he was recently elected mayor of Richmond—and is currently involved in developing a civil rights museum. In 2002, Leroy R. Hassell, Sr., became chief justice of the Virginia Supreme Court, the first African-American to hold that post and the first to be elected by his fellow justices.

Over the last few years, the Virginia Foundation for the Humanities has joined forces with the Virginia Tourism Corporation to produce the African-American Heritage Program as

Arthur Ashe. A native of Richmond, Va., he was ranked America's number one tennis player in 1969, a prestige he used to help bring an end to apartheid in South Africa. In 1995, his statue was added, amid controversy, to the famed series of statues of Confederate heroes of the Civil War on Monument Avenu in the Fan District.
CREDIT: Virginia Historical Society

an "educational and economic resource for the Commonwealth."[6] Its purpose is to encourage tourists to visit African-American historical sites throughout the state. Moreover, the General Assembly has awarded funding to develop a database of black history with emphasis on historic sites.[7]

Virginia today recognizes the long-overlooked contributions of its African-American citizenry and seeks to celebrate that heritage through programs and museums located throughout the Commonwealth. The twin goals of this program—to promote education and the Old Dominion's economy—are not so different from those pursued by Virginia's founding fathers, principally Jefferson and Madison, who struggled to find a secure economic base for their state and nation even as they pushed for public education, believing it to be central to the survival of the republic. The solution to slavery which eluded them was resolved in the civil war they feared might one day tear the country apart. But the Union survived and so did the state they loved so well.

Notes

1. "Colored" was the term used to apply to black and Indian peoples alike; a reference to anyone not white. It cast a wide net of discrimination and led to many light-skinned people attempting to "pass"—that is leave family behind and pretend to be white. This was particularly true among Indian peoples in the South. In some areas where black and Indian peoples had intermarried, their descendents claimed Indian identity in a futile effort to find some heightened status in this closed society.
2. See R. C. Smith, *They Closed Their Schools: Prince Edward County, Virginia, 1951–1964* (Farmville, Martha E. Forrester Council of Women, 1966). See also Robbins L. Gates, *The Making of Massive Resistance: Virginia's Politics of Public School Desegregation, 1954–1956* (Chapel Hill: University of North Carolina Press, 1964).

3. Lacy Ward, Jr., *On Establishing the Robert Russa Moton Museum: National Sites Which Serve as Examples* (Thesis prepared for Degree of Master of Public Administration, Virginia Polytechnic Institute and State University, 1999), 3.
4. "Negroes Urged to Action in Prince Edward," *Richmond Times Dispatch* (September 23, 1964), 1:3–2:1,2. One of the factors that still irk people who lived through this period of school closure is that public property taxes, ostensibly for public education use, continued to be collected during those years.
5. "Civil Rights in Education Heritage Trail receives TEA Funding," 1999 Annual Report, Old Dominion Resource Conservation & Development. The RCD Council may be contacted at 250 LeGrande Avenue, Suite F; Charlottesville, VA 23923. For more information about current activities at the Moton Museum, visit www.moton.org.
6. "African-American History in Virginia," A Brochure produced by the Virginia Foundation for the Humanities. For more information about this program, please visit their Web site at www.virginia.edu/vfh.
7. To access the database, visit www.virginia.edu/vfh/aahv/data.html.

Epilogue

On September 11, 2001, Virginia, like New York, came under attack as one of the four airplanes hijacked that day slammed into the Pentagon. So many died; no one in America remained untouched by the largest attack on the United States since Pearl Harbor. Some of the students on the campus where I teach lost a parent or a brother in those horrors. All were stunned, grieving, and looking to their professors, most of whom, like this one, were also too young to have any experience of war, much less an attack on American soil.

Today, the docks at the Norfolk Naval Base seem so empty, a stark visual reminder that this nation is once again at war. Many reservists among my students have already been called away. But this country has come through battle before and Virginia, in particular, has borne witness to war's harsh realities. This state has seen hard times; still harder may be yet to come. But as I write these words, it is once again springtime in Virginia. The dogwoods are in bloom; the honeysuckle has begun to blossom. The beauty of this land, which led so many Indian peoples to call it home for thousands of years and drew the first English settlers to these shores four hundred years ago, is so abundantly evident. In the Shenandoah, Virginia's horses continue to graze. This summer, the Chincoteague ponies will once again swim.

Virginia, where so much of the past meets the present, possesses a timeless quality. There is also a legacy left by the brave people who have lived here, from George Washington, commander of a ragtag Continental Army that withstood the might of the British Empire, to Barbara Johns, a teenager whose actions would help transform a nation two centuries later. From Robert E. Lee, who sought to find honor defending a cause he knew was wrong, to Booker T. Washington and L. Francis Griffith, who bound the wounds left by generations of slavery—these Virginians left us the courage of their example and their vision of America.

At some point, all Americans should visit Virginia. Walk up the mountain to Thomas Jefferson's Monticello as Edgar Allan Poe did in 1826; wander through the hallways of the Robert Russa Moton School; trek the Appalachian Trail through the Blue Ridge; stand where Patrick Henry did when he exhorted his fellow colonists to seek their liberty; gaze at the rolling hillsides of Arlington and Hollywood Cemeteries, their memorials a lasting promise that Americans will not forget. Virginia's past, a capsule of American history, surrounds one at every turn in the Old Dominion, reminding us of the United States' beginnings and committing us to its future.

Bibliography

Allen, W. B., ed. *George Washington: A Collection*. Indianapolis: Liberty Classics, 1989.

Andrews, Matthew Page. *Virginia: The Old Dominion*. Richmond: The Dietz Press, 1949.

"Anti-Slavery Petitions Presented to the Virginia Legislature." *Journal of Negro History*. (1927) 12: 671–673.

Badenhop, Robert; Kathryn Blackwell, Kathleen Costello, Jason Knause, Sherry L. Livingston, Robyn Olson-Goodman, Sandra Pleva, Megan E. Wade, and Wahlgren. *Longwood: A Campus and a Community*. A Project of the Longwood University Public History Program, available on compact disc, 2001.

Coski, John M. and Amy R. Feely. "A Monument to Southern Womanhood: The Founding Generation of the Confederate Museum" in *A Woman's War: Southern Women, Civil War and the Confederate Legacy,* Edward D. C. Campbell, Jr., ed. Charlottesville: University of Virginia Press, 1997.

Dabney, Virginius. *Virginia: A New Dominion*. New York: Doubleday and Company, 1971.

Daniel, J. R. V., ed. *A Hornbook of Virginia History*. Richmond: Virginia Department of Conservation and Development, 1949.

Eliot, Jonathan. *The Debates of the Several State Conventions*. Philadelphia: Lippincott, 1937.

Ellis, Joseph. *American Sphinx: The Character of Thomas Jefferson*. New York: Alfred A. Knopf, 1997.

Faust, Drew Gilbert. *Mothers of Invention: Women of the Slave-holding South.* New York: Vintage, 1997.

Ferrand, Max, ed. *The Records of the Federalist Convention of 1787.* New Haven: Yale University Press, 1937.

Foner, Eric. *Free Soil, Free Labor, Free Men.* New York: Oxford University Press, 1995.

Gordon-Reid, Annette. *Thomas Jefferson and Sally Hemings.* Charlottesville: University of Virginia Press, 1998.

Heights, Dorothy I. *Open Wide the Freedom Gates: A Memoir.* Public Affairs, 2003.

Holt, Michael. *The Political Crises of the 1850s.* New York: W. W. Norton and Company, 1983.

Hosmer, Charles B. Jr. *Presence of the Past: A History of the Preservation Movement in the United States before Williamsburg.* Washington: National Trust for Historic Preservation, 1965.

Hume, Ivor Noel. *The Virginia Adventure: Roanoke to James Towne.* New York: Alfred A. Knopf, 1994.

Jefferson, Thomas. *Notes on the State of Virginia.* David Waldstreicher, ed. Boston: Bedford/St. Martin's Press, 2002.

Kettner, James H. *The Development of American Citizenship, 1608–1870.* Chapel Hill: University of North Carolina Press, 1984.

Kingsbury, Susan Myra, ed. *The Records of the Virginia Land Company.* Washington: Government Printing Office, 1906.

Kinnear, Duncan Lyle. *The First 100 Years: A History of Virginia Polytechnic Institute and State University.* Blacksburg: VPI Educational Foundation, 1972.

Korngold, Ralph. "Woe If It Comes with Storm and Blood and Fire." *Portraits of America.* Stephen B. Oates, ed. Boston: Houghton Mifflin Company, 1991.

McColley, Robert. *Slavery and Jeffersonian Virginia.* Champaign: University of Illinois Press, 1964.

McGinnis, Carol. *Virginia Genealogy: Sources and Resources.* Baltimore: Genealogical Publishing Company, 1993.

McPherson, James M. *Battle Cry of Freedom: The Civil War Era.* New York: Oxford University Press, 2003.

———. *For Cause and Comrade: Why Men Fought in the Civil War.* New York: Oxford University Press, 1998.

Mitchell, Mary. *Hollywood Cemetery: The History of a Southern Shrine.* Richmond: Virginia State Library, 1999.

Morgan, Edmund. *American Slavery, American Freedom: The Ordeal of Colonial Virginia.* New York: W. W. Norton and Company, 1995.

"Negroes Urged to Action in Prince Edward." *Richmond Times-Dispatch* (September 23, 1964).

Peterson, Merrill D. *Jefferson Image in the American Mind.* New York: Oxford University Press, 1992.

Potter, David Morris. *Impending Crisis.* New York: Perennial Press, 1977.

Robertson, James I., Jr. *Civil War Sites in Virginia: A Tour Guide.* Charlottesville: University of Virginia Press, 1982.

———. *General A. P. Hill: The Story of a Confederate Warrior.* New York: Random House, 1987.

———. *Soldiers Blue and Gray.* Columbia: University of South Carolina Press, 1998.

———. *Standing Like a Stone Wall: The Life of General Thomas J. Jackson.* Atheneum Books, 2001.

Robson, David W. *Educating Republicans: The College in the Era of the American Revolution, 1750–1800.* New York: Greenwood Press, 1985.

Smith, John. *The generall historie of Virginia, New England and the Summer Isles, together with the true travels, adventures and observations, and A sea Grammar, by Captain John Smith.* Glasgow: J. MacLehose, 1907.

Smith, R.C. *They Closed Their Schools: Prince Edward County, Virginia, 1951–1964.* Farmville: Martha E. Forrester Council of Women, 1966.

Virginia Writer's Project (WPA). *Virginia: A Guide to the Old Dominion.* New York: Oxford University Press, 1940.

Wallerstein, Peter. *Virginia Tech: Land-Grant University.* Blacksburg: Pocahontas Press, 1997.

Ward, Lacey, Jr. *On Establishing the Robert Russa Moton Museum: National Sites Which Serve as Examples.* Thesis for Degree of Master of Public Administration, Virginia Polytechnic Institute and State University, 1999.

Washington, Booker T. *Up From Slavery: An Autobiography.* New York: Dover Publications, 1995 (first published in 1907).

West, Patricia. *Domesticating History: The Political Origins of America's House Museums.* Washington: Smithsonian Institution Press, 1999.

Wiley, Bell I. *Confederate Women.* New York: Greenwood Publishing, 1975.

Wood, Gordon. *The Creation of the American Republic, 1776–1787.* New York: W.W. Norton and Company, 1969.

Wyatt-Brown, Bertram. *The House of Percy: Honor, Melancholy, and Imagination in a Southern Family.* New York: Oxford University Press, 1994.

Websites of Interest

For a photographic tour of Virginia plantations and historic sites including its battlefields:
>   www.virginia.org.

For a visual tour of Monticello:
>   www.monticello.org.

For information about African-American history sites and the Civil Rights Trail:
>   www.virginia.edu/vfh.

To access the database of Black History Documents:
>   www.virginia.edu/vfh/aahv/data.html.

For information about the Robert Russa Moton Museum:
>   www.moton.org.

To learn more about the current restoration work being undertaken at James Madison's Home:
>   www.montpelier.org.

For a wealth of photographs of the many monuments to "The Lost Cause" and "Our Glorious Dead" contained in Hollywood Cemetery in Richmond:
>   www.historicrichmond.com/hollywood.html.

For a virtual tour of Colonial Williamsburg:
>   www.colonialwilliamsburg.com.

Index